NATURE

Written by
**Neil Ardley, Michael Chinery,
Jennifer Cochrane and Jeanette Harris**

Illustrated by
**Stephen Adams, Graham Allen, Trevor Boyer,
Ian Garrard, Alan Male, Bernard Robinson,
John Thompson, Fred'k St Ward,
Mike Woodhatch and David Wright**

A Piccolo Explorer Book

Contents

INTRODUCTION

THIS BOOK is your passport to the amazing world of nature. Birds and mammals, shells and insects, trees and flowers – all are fascinating in their different ways. Each of the book's chapters tells you about one of them, and many drawings help identify what you see.

Birds are very easy to spot, even in a town, especially if you attract them to your windows with food. Mammals are much shyer, but you can often see creatures like the hedgehog and grey squirrel, although badgers and otters are much rarer. Insects are all around us in many shapes and sizes – from the gardener's friend, the ladybird – to the much-disliked housefly. Many beaches are dotted with lovely shells, and wild flowers splash field and hedgerow with colour. Above them all are the lordly trees, home and food for so many creatures.

Below, left to right: Bluebell, common mallow, marsh marigold, foxglove, creeping jenny (bottom centre), lesser bindweed, periwinkle (bottom right), wood anemone (top right).

WILD FLOWERS

All around you in the countryside – and even in odd corners in the town – there are many lovely wild flowers to see and enjoy. The next few pages will help you identify many of the commoner ones. Labels beside each drawing of a plant tell you its main time for flowering, and give information on the type of place where you might find it.

You can, of course, pick a few of the commoner wild flowers and press them for a flower collection, but it is really much better to leave them growing where they are. Then other people will see and enjoy them, too. You will get just as much fun from simply finding and identifying them – without picking them and bringing them home to die, especially as some flowers are now quite scarce.

What to Look For

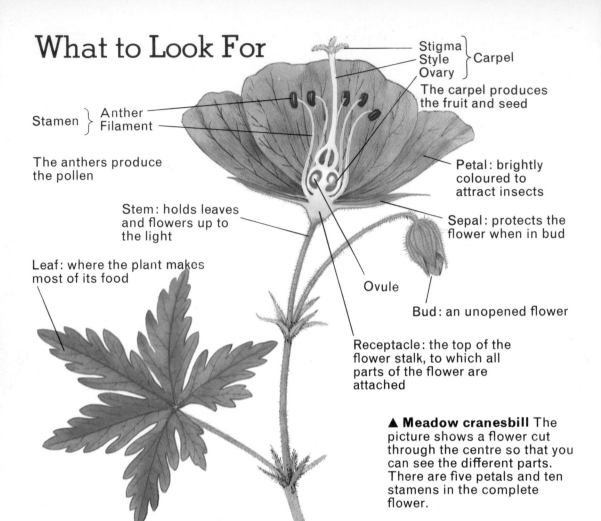

Stigma
Style ⎫ Carpel
Ovary ⎭

The carpel produces
the fruit and seed

Stamen ⎫ Anther
⎬ Filament

The anthers produce
the pollen

Petal: brightly
coloured to
attract insects

Stem: holds leaves
and flowers up to
the light

Sepal: protects the
flower when in bud

Leaf: where the plant makes
most of its food

Ovule

Bud: an unopened flower

Receptacle: the top of the
flower stalk, to which all
parts of the flower are
attached

▲ **Meadow cranesbill** The
picture shows a flower cut
through the centre so that you
can see the different parts.
There are five petals and ten
stamens in the complete
flower.

Wild flowers can be found more or less everywhere – in towns as well as in the countryside. Most of them are very attractive and quite easy to recognize. When the plants are not in flower, you can often recognize them by their leaves. But leaves can vary quite a lot according to where the plant is growing. Plants growing in shady places often have bigger leaves than ones growing in the open. The plants in shady places are often taller as well.

The flowers of one kind of plant can vary in size, but they are almost always made up in the same way. Look first for the number of *petals* – most flowers have four, five, or six. Sometimes they are all alike; sometimes they have different shapes. In some flowers they are joined together to form a tube. Count the numbers of *sepals*, *stamens* and *stigmas* as well. Flowers with similar structures are grouped together to form families.

Poppy

Harebell

Vetch

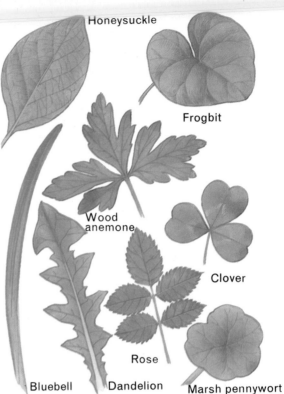

Honeysuckle

Frogbit

Wood anemone

Clover

Rose

Bluebell

Dandelion

Marsh pennywort

Flowers are of many different shapes. The poppy has four separate petals which are all alike. The harebell has five petals all joined together. The petals of the vetch are of different shapes. The corn marigold is a composite flower: dozens of tiny flowers in one head.

Corn marigold

What Flowers Are For

The job of the flower is to produce *seeds*, from which new plants can grow. Seeds develop from the *ovules* in the *carpels* after the flower has been pollinated. *Pollination* means the transfer of pollen from the stamens to the stigmas. Wind or insects usually carry pollen from one flower to another. You should not pick too many flowers. If you do, there will not be enough seeds to make new plants for the future.

Leaves have many different shapes, as shown above. Those of the rose, the wood anemone, and the clover are divided into separate leaflets. They are compound leaves. The arrangement on the stem also varies. Four different arrangements are shown below.

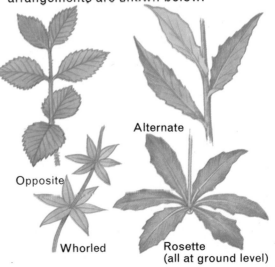

Alternate

Opposite

Whorled

Rosette (all at ground level)

7

Keeping a Record

A notebook and pencil are essential if you are going to make a proper study of wild flowers. A lens or magnifying glass is also very useful. Make drawings of the flowers you find. Make drawings of the leaves too, or else pick a leaf and press it or make a rubbing (see opposite). Write down all the information you can, such as the date, the place where you find each plant and the height of the plant. Look at the soil and write down whether it is sandy, chalky, heavy clay and so on. Is the plant growing in the shade or in the open? You will soon see from your record book that not all flowers live everywhere. Many, such as the alpine gentian (page 16), are very fussy where they live. Others live almost anywhere and many of these become *weeds* in our gardens.

You can pick some of the commoner flowers and press them, but never pick a flower if you can see only a few of its kind. It might be very rare. Never dig up wild flowers.

▼ **A page** from your flower record book might look like this. The drawing clearly shows what the actual plant (below left) looks like. See if you can find this flower in this book. In what sort of place does it live?

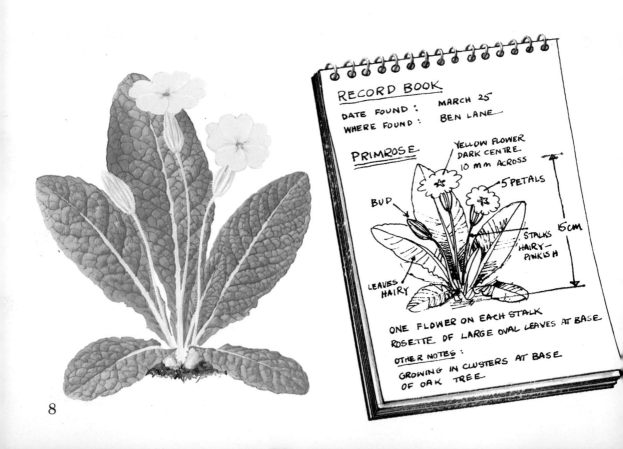

RECORD BOOK

DATE FOUND : MARCH 25

WHERE FOUND : BEN LANE

PRIMROSE

YELLOW FLOWER DARK CENTRE 10 mm ACROSS

5 PETALS

BUD

STALKS 15 cm HAIRY - PINKISH

LEAVES HAIRY

ONE FLOWER ON EACH STALK

ROSETTE OF LARGE OVAL LEAVES AT BASE

OTHER NOTES :

GROWING IN CLUSTERS AT BASE OF OAK TREE

◀ **Flower press** You can make a simple flower press with two pieces of plywood or hardboard, two straps and some sheets of blotting paper. Put the flowers between the blotting paper sheets and strap the boards firmly round them. The holes in the wood are not essential but they speed up the drying process. The flowers should be quite dry in two weeks and you can then mount them in your record book as shown below.
If you cannot make a press, put your flowers between blotting paper under a pile of heavy books.

Leaves can be pressed in just the same way as flowers. You can also make leaf rubbings. Put a leaf on a flat surface and cover it with a sheet of paper. Hold everything firmly in place and rub a crayon over the leaf area. The details of the leaf surface will show up clearly on the paper.

▼ **A flower record book** with pressed flowers, drawings, notes and a photograph.

RED CAMPION

DATE FOUND: MAY 10.
WHERE FOUND: HOUND WOOD
NOTES: LEAVES SOFT, HAIRY
         BASE OF LOWER LEAVES ELONGATED

LEAVES   FLOWER

Woodland Flowers

If you walk through a *deciduous* woodland in spring you will usually find a rich carpet of flowers on the ground. The deciduous trees, such as the oak and the ash, drop their leaves for the winter. Plenty of sunlight can thus reach the woodland floor in early spring before the new tree leaves are fully grown. Low-growing plants can flourish at this time, but many die down as the tree leaves open out and cut off the light. All plants need light to make food and grow. Very few small plants can grow in *evergreen* woodlands. This is because the pines and other cone-bearing trees keep their leaves all the year round. Very little light ever reaches the ground. Flowering plants are generally restricted to the woodland margins and to clearings.

▶ **Early purple orchid**
Spring, mainly in damp places.

▲ **Yellow archangel**
Late spring, usually on heavy soil.

▼ **Wood spurge** Spring, usually in damp woods. Up to 1 metre high.

▶ **Wood forget-me-not**
Spring and summer, mainly in damp woods.

◀ **Bluebell** Spring, often carpeting large areas of woodland floor.

◀ **Primrose**
Spring, in hedgerows as well as woods.

▶ **Bird's nest orchid** Early summer, in deep shade, often in beech woods.

▲ **Early dog violet**
Early spring, in woods and hedgerows.

Some White Woodland Flowers

▲ **White helleborine**
Summer, in shade and on lime-rich soils.

▲ **Wood anemone**
Spring. It has up to 9 petals.

▲ **Lily of the valley** Late spring, in dry woods.

▲ **Wood sorrel**
Spring, in very shady places.

▲ **Wild strawberry**
Spring and early summer.

▲ **Dog's mercury**
Early spring, carpets ground.

▲ **Snowdrop**
Winter and early spring, in damp woods.

▲ **Solomon's seal**
Late spring, often in dense patches.

▼ **Herb Bennet** Summer. Up to 60 cm high. Fruits hooked.

▶ **Foxglove** Summer in woodland clearings. Up to 1·5 metres high.

◀ **Herb Paris**
Late spring, on lime-rich soils. Rare.

▶ **Stinking hellebore**
Winter and spring, in dry woods mainly on lime-rich soils.

▶ **Bugle** Spring, mainly in damp woods. Creeps over ground.

▲ **Lesser celandine**
Spring, in woods and hedgerows. Up to 12 petals.

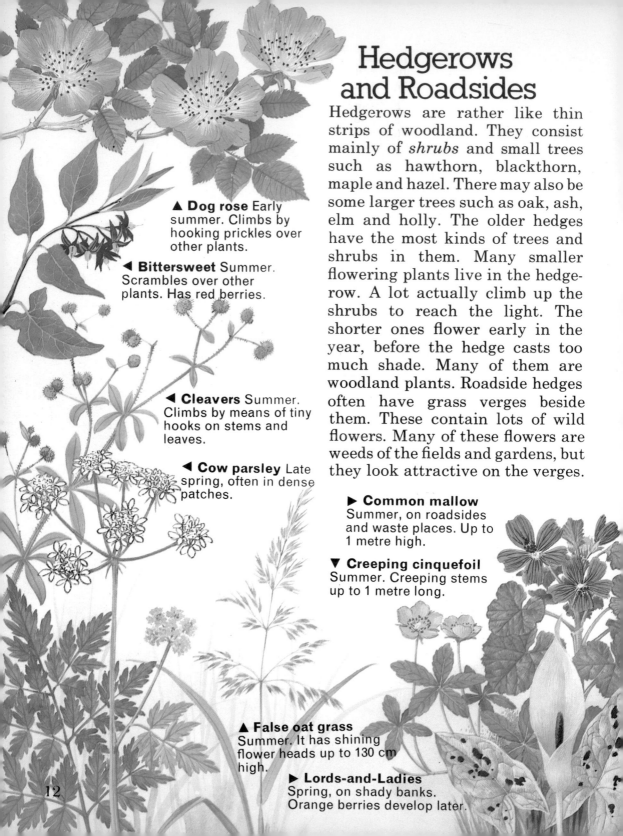

Hedgerows and Roadsides

Hedgerows are rather like thin strips of woodland. They consist mainly of *shrubs* and small trees such as hawthorn, blackthorn, maple and hazel. There may also be some larger trees such as oak, ash, elm and holly. The older hedges have the most kinds of trees and shrubs in them. Many smaller flowering plants live in the hedgerow. A lot actually climb up the shrubs to reach the light. The shorter ones flower early in the year, before the hedge casts too much shade. Many of them are woodland plants. Roadside hedges often have grass verges beside them. These contain lots of wild flowers. Many of these flowers are weeds of the fields and gardens, but they look attractive on the verges.

▲ **Dog rose** Early summer. Climbs by hooking prickles over other plants.

◀ **Bittersweet** Summer. Scrambles over other plants. Has red berries.

◀ **Cleavers** Summer. Climbs by means of tiny hooks on stems and leaves.

◀ **Cow parsley** Late spring, often in dense patches.

▶ **Common mallow** Summer, on roadsides and waste places. Up to 1 metre high.

▼ **Creeping cinquefoil** Summer. Creeping stems up to 1 metre long.

▲ **False oat grass** Summer. It has shining flower heads up to 130 cm high.

▶ **Lords-and-Ladies** Spring, on shady banks. Orange berries develop later.

▼ Hedge bindweed
Summer. Twines over
other hedgerow plants.

▶ Honeysuckle
Summer. Twines
around other shrubs.

▼ White bryony
Summer. Climbs with
coiled, spring-like
tendrils.

▶ Blackberry
Summer. Climbs by
means of prickles.

▲ Hogweed Spring
and summer. Flowers
white or pink.

▲ Tufted vetch
Summer. Climbs with
branched tendrils.

▲ White deadnettle
Spring to autumn, on
hedgebanks and waste
ground.

▶ Common teasel
Summer. Very prickly.
Dead heads stand
throughout winter.

◀ Chicory Summer, on
grass verges.

▶ Cotton thistle
Summer, on bare
ground, especially
sandy.

13

Fields and Meadows

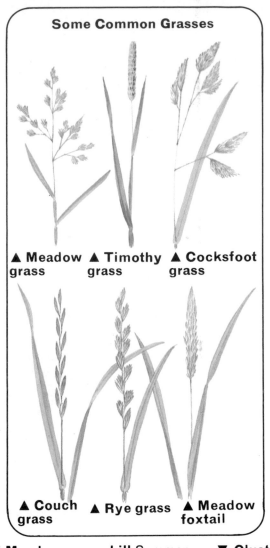

Some Common Grasses

▲ Meadow grass

▲ Timothy grass

▲ Cocksfoot grass

▲ Couch grass

▲ Rye grass

▲ Meadow foxtail

Fields which are regularly grazed by animals do not contain many flowers. Only the grasses and a few other plants can stand the constant nibbling. Meadows, in which the grasses are allowed to grow up for hay, contain more flowers. Many meadows are ploughed up every few years and sown with special seed mixtures to produce the best hay. These meadows contain little apart from the grasses and clovers with which they are sown.

The best places for wild flowers are the open hillsides, especially in chalk and limestone regions. Roadside banks are also very good for grassland flowers. Several attractive flowers, such as the poppy, like disturbed soil. They often grow as weeds in corn fields. Couch grass is another weed, very common on roadside verges. The other grasses shown on the left are valuable and they are regularly grown in hay meadows.

▼ **Meadow cranesbill** Summer, usually on limestone.

▼ **Clustered bellflower** Summer and autumn, on limestone.

▼ **Wild clary** Summer, in dry grassy places.

▼ **Common milkwort** Summer, on grassy banks and hillsides.

▼ **Common field speedwell** All year round, in cultivated fields and gardens.

▶ **Broomrape** Summer, on fields and grassy banks.

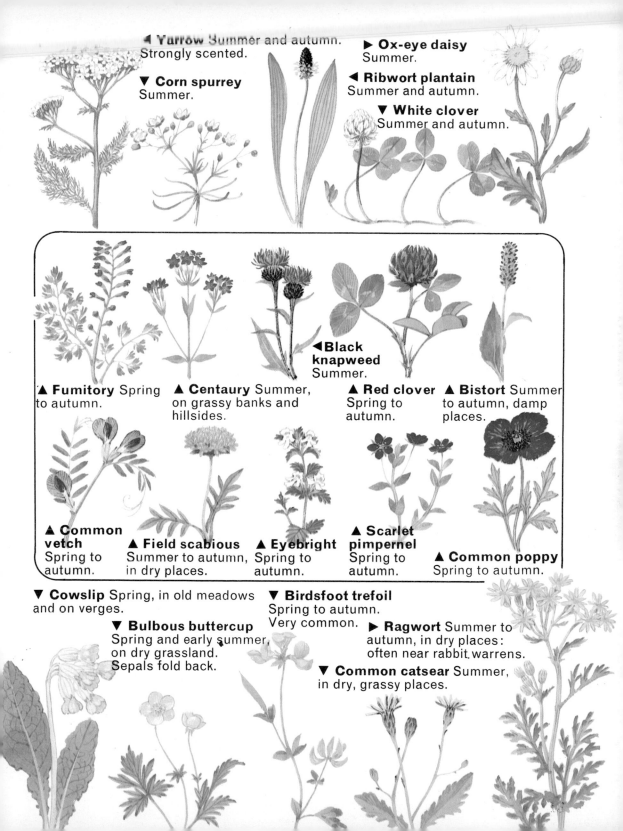

◀ **Yarrow** Summer and autumn. Strongly scented.

▼ **Corn spurrey** Summer.

▶ **Ox-eye daisy** Summer.

◀ **Ribwort plantain** Summer and autumn.

▼ **White clover** Summer and autumn.

◀**Black knapweed** Summer.

▲ **Fumitory** Spring to autumn.

▲ **Centaury** Summer, on grassy banks and hillsides.

▲ **Red clover** Spring to autumn.

▲ **Bistort** Summer to autumn, damp places.

▲ **Common vetch** Spring to autumn.

▲ **Field scabious** Summer to autumn, in dry places.

▲ **Eyebright** Spring to autumn.

▲ **Scarlet pimpernel** Spring to autumn.

▲ **Common poppy** Spring to autumn.

▼ **Cowslip** Spring, in old meadows and on verges.

▼ **Bulbous buttercup** Spring and early summer, on dry grassland. Sepals fold back.

▼ **Birdsfoot trefoil** Spring to autumn. Very common.

▶ **Ragwort** Summer to autumn, in dry places: often near rabbit warrens.

▼ **Common catsear** Summer, in dry, grassy places.

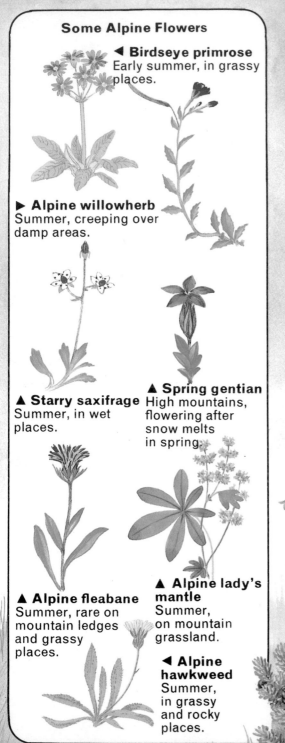

Some Alpine Flowers

◄ Birdseye primrose
Early summer, in grassy places.

► Alpine willowherb
Summer, creeping over damp areas.

▲ Starry saxifrage
Summer, in wet places.

▲ Spring gentian
High mountains, flowering after snow melts in spring.

▲ Alpine fleabane
Summer, rare on mountain ledges and grassy places.

▲ Alpine lady's mantle
Summer, on mountain grassland.

◄ Alpine hawkweed
Summer, in grassy and rocky places.

Heaths, Moors and Mountains

A heath is an area of poor, sandy soil. It is usually covered with dwarf shrubs such as ling and bell heather. These are both members of the family of plants which are also called heaths. Gorse and broom also grow on heathlands. In wet areas the sand may be covered with *peat*. Insect-trapping plants such as the sundew may grow on the peat.

Peat-covered areas on high ground are called moors. They are covered by various grasses and members of the heath family. High mountains are very cold and windy. Only short plants can grow there. They are called alpine plants. Most of them form dense cushions or mats of leaves at ground level. The leaves are often waxy or hairy.

◄Harebell Summer to autumn, on dry heaths and grasslands.

► Sundew Wet places. Tiny flowers appear in summer. Flies are trapped by the sticky leaves.

► Cotton-grass Waterlogged heaths and moors (bogs). The 'cotton' carries seeds away in summer.

▲ Crowberry Tiny pink flowers in spring, and then black berries.

The Heath Family

▲ **Ling** Summer. Very common on both wet and dry heaths.

▲ **Bell heather** Early summer to autumn, on dry heaths and moors.

▲ **Cross-leaved heath** Summer to autumn, on wet heaths and moors. Leaves in fours.

▲ **Bilberry** Flowers spring to early summer on heaths and moors.

▲ **Cowberry** Flowers spring and early summer. An evergreen mainly on moors.

▲ **Cranberry** Pointed pink flowers in summer. Creeps over bogs and wet heaths.

◀ **Butterwort** Early summer, in waterlogged areas. Catches insects on sticky leaves.

▶ **Gorse** Flowers all year on heaths and other places. Very spiny.

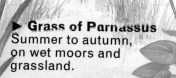

▶ **Grass of Parnassus** Summer to autumn, on wet moors and grassland.

◀ **Bog asphodel** Summer, on wet heaths and bogs.

▶ **Broom** Spring, on dry heathland. No spines.

17

Seashore Flowers

Flowering plants normally grow only above the highest tide levels. You will find them on the cliffs and sand dunes. You will also find a few on the shingle banks. Long roots hold the plants firmly among the shifting stones. All seaside plants have to be able to stand large amounts of salt. They are called halophytes, which means 'salt-lovers'.

Salt marshes are flat, muddy areas generally found around river mouths. They are covered by the highest tides, but they do support quite a number of flowering plants. Many of these have thick, fleshy leaves. Sea-lavender is especially common. Its flowers turn the salt marshes purple in summer.

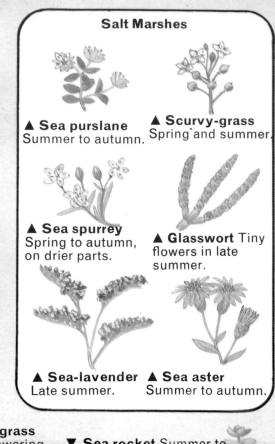

Salt Marshes

▲ **Sea purslane** Summer to autumn.

▲ **Scurvy-grass** Spring and summer.

▲ **Sea spurrey** Spring to autumn, on drier parts.

▲ **Glasswort** Tiny flowers in late summer.

▲ **Sea-lavender** Late summer.

▲ **Sea aster** Summer to autumn.

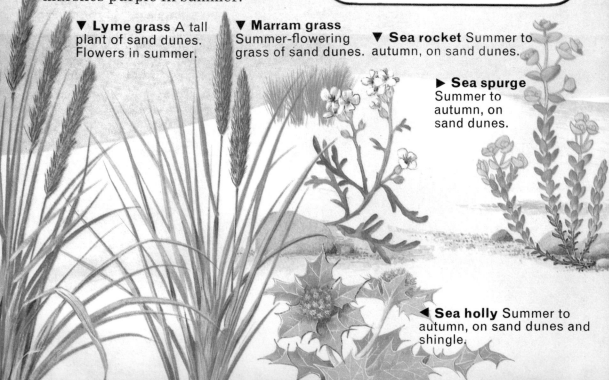

▼ **Lyme grass** A tall plant of sand dunes. Flowers in summer.

▼ **Marram grass** Summer-flowering grass of sand dunes.

▼ **Sea rocket** Summer to autumn, on sand dunes.

▶ **Sea spurge** Summer to autumn, on sand dunes.

◀ **Sea holly** Summer to autumn, on sand dunes and shingle.

Shingle Beaches

▲ **Sea pea** Summer. It has fleshy stems.

▲ **Sea kale** Summer, on sand as well as shingle.

▲ **Yellow horned poppy** Summer.

▶ **Hottentot fig** Spring and summer, on cliffs and dunes. Dark pink, white or yellow.

▶ **Thrift** Spring to late summer, on cliffs and saltmarshes.

▼ **Sea campion** Summer, on cliffs and shingle.

▼ **Rock samphire** Summer to autumn, on cliffs and dunes.

◀ **Shrubby seablite** Summer to autumn, on sand and shingle.

▶ **Viper's bugloss** Spring to autumn, on sand dunes.

◀ **Sea beet** Summer, on all kinds of shores.

▲ **Sea bindweed** Summer and early autumn, usually on sand dunes.

▲ **Prickly saltwort** Summer to autumn, creeping over sand.

Ponds, Streams and Marshes

◀ **Flowering rush** Summer, in shallow water.

▼ **Yellow iris** Summer, in marshy ground and pond margins.

Lots of flowers grow in or near water. Those at the water's edge, with just their roots in the water, are called emergent plants. Submerged plants grow right under the water. But others, like the water lilies, have floating leaves. The flowers are almost always above the surface. Most water plants are rooted to the bottom, but some float freely in the water. The stems of submerged and floating plants do not need to be very strong because they are held up by the water. They usually collapse if removed from the water. Marsh plants are those that grow in waterlogged ground, where the water-level is very near the surface.

▼ **Marestail** In shallow water. Tiny pink flowers in summer.

▼ **Water soldier** Summer. Sinks to the bottom when flowering is over.

▼ **Water crowfoot** Spring to autumn, in ponds and streams.

▲ **Bulrush** The furry brown flower spikes can be seen most of the year around the edges of ponds.

▲ **Great willowherb** Summer, by stream banks, ditches and marshy ground.

▲ **Branched bur-reed** Summer, at edges of ponds and streams.

▲ **Canadian pondweed** Submerged in ponds and slow-moving streams. Flowers very rarely.

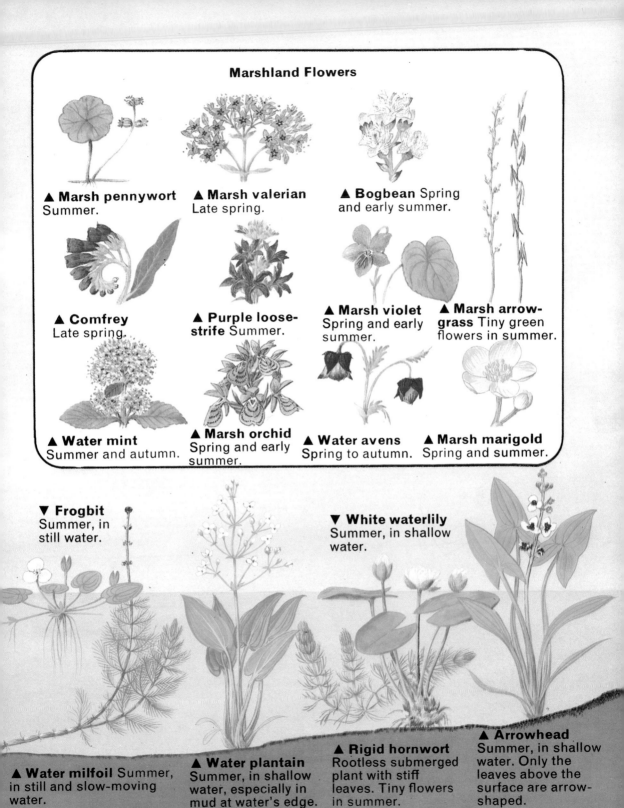

Marshland Flowers

▲ **Marsh pennywort** Summer.

▲ **Marsh valerian** Late spring.

▲ **Bogbean** Spring and early summer.

▲ **Comfrey** Late spring.

▲ **Purple loose-strife** Summer.

▲ **Marsh violet** Spring and early summer.

▲ **Marsh arrow-grass** Tiny green flowers in summer.

▲ **Water mint** Summer and autumn.

▲ **Marsh orchid** Spring and early summer.

▲ **Water avens** Spring to autumn.

▲ **Marsh marigold** Spring and summer.

▼ **Frogbit** Summer, in still water.

▼ **White waterlily** Summer, in shallow water.

▲ **Water milfoil** Summer, in still and slow-moving water.

▲ **Water plantain** Summer, in shallow water, especially in mud at water's edge.

▲ **Rigid hornwort** Rootless submerged plant with stiff leaves. Tiny flowers in summer.

▲ **Arrowhead** Summer, in shallow water. Only the leaves above the surface are arrow-shaped.

Town Flowers

All flowers produce seeds which are scattered by the wind or by animals. The seeds start to grow when they reach suitable places. Many seeds find their way into towns where they find plenty of places in which to grow. They take root on waste ground and railway yards, in pavement cracks and on old walls, and in town gardens. Many of the plants shown on these two pages have light, fluffy seeds that are easily blown by wind.

Most of these plants are called weeds when they occur in gardens, but they can look very pretty on old walls and in waste places. Plants with heavier seeds which do not travel far in the wind may reach towns by spreading along railway banks and roadsides.

Many of the plants that spring up in towns are 'foreigners'. Some are cultivated plants whose seeds have escaped from gardens. Many others are brought in as seeds on the clothing of travellers or in imported produce.

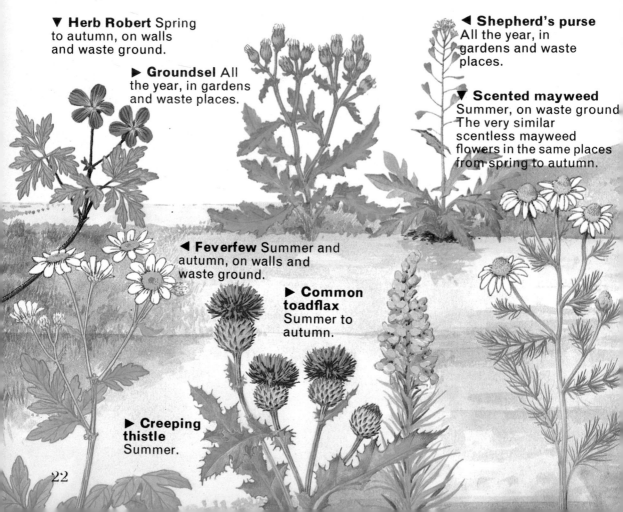

▼ **Herb Robert** Spring to autumn, on walls and waste ground.

▶ **Groundsel** All the year, in gardens and waste places.

◀ **Shepherd's purse** All the year, in gardens and waste places.

▼ **Scented mayweed** Summer, on waste ground. The very similar scentless mayweed flowers in the same places from spring to autumn.

◀ **Feverfew** Summer and autumn, on walls and waste ground.

▶ **Common toadflax** Summer to autumn.

▶ **Creeping thistle** Summer.

◄ Rosebay willowherb
Summer and autumn, on walls and waste ground, especially after fire.

► Wallflower
Spring and early summer.

▼ Ivy-leaved toadflax
Spring to autumn.

▼ Oxford ragwort
Spring to autumn.

▲ White stonecrop
Summer, on walls.

▼ White campion
Spring to autumn, in gardens and on bare ground.

▼ Greater celandine
Spring to autumn, on waste ground, especially around walls.

▼ Dandelion Flowers most of the year on lawns and waste ground.

◄ Daisy Flowers all the year on lawns and waste ground.

Below, from left to right: Norway spruce female flower and cone; leaves of dwarf fan palm; catkins and nuts of hazel; flowers and fruits of hawthorn; and leaves and fruits of the fig.

TREES

Trees grow almost everywhere on Earth, except for the very coldest and driest places. You can see them all around you — in parks and gardens, hedgerows and, of course, in woodlands. Trees play a very important role in nature, for they provide food and shelter for an immense number of birds and other animals. Just think of the thousands of acorns scattered by an oak tree — and the jays and squirrels that eagerly bury them for food.

The next chapter will help you to recognize some of the commoner trees from their leaves, flowers and fruits. You will also discover some of the fascinating things that happen to a tree round the year, and learn how to guess its height and age. Best of all, you can learn how to make a record of what you discover.

What to Look For

Trees can be studied at any time, even in the depths of winter when many of them have lost their leaves. Each kind or species has its own distinctive bark pattern, and with a little practice you can recognize most species from their bark. The appearance of the winter buds is also a good clue.

The shape of the whole tree may be a useful guide when the tree is growing alone in a park or a hedge-row, but trees growing close together in a wood rarely get the chance to develop their full shape.

From late spring until autumn, you will have leaves to help you identify trees, and at certain times of the year, flowers. Fruits and seeds, generally found in summer or autumn, are equally useful. Notice also what sort of ground the trees grow in. Some kinds, for instance the crack willow, grow only in wet ground, while others, such as the Scot's pine, require well-drained soils.

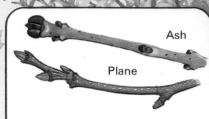

Ash

Plane

Buds The winter buds contain the next season's leaves and in some cases flowers as well.

Branches contain many tiny tubes which carry water and minerals to the leaves and food away from them.

Cherry   Pine

Bark The dead and cracked outer bark protects the living trunk beneath.

Most conifers are shaped like a triangle because the main trunk keeps growing upwards. Broad-leaved trees usually fork and fan out, so they are rounder.

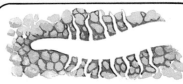

Roots anchor the tree in the ground. The root hairs absorb water and minerals in the soil.

26

Sycamore

Rowan

Sweet chestnut

Silver fir

Leaves are where the tree makes its food. Deciduous leaves fall in the autumn, but evergreen leaves remain throughout the year. Cone-bearing trees, such as the silver fir, usually have needle-like leaves but flowering trees generally have broad leaves.

1

2

3

4

Flowers Some trees, such as horse chestnut (1), have large, attractive flowers. The alder (2) and oak (3) have small ones bunched into catkins. The Scot's pine (4) has cones.

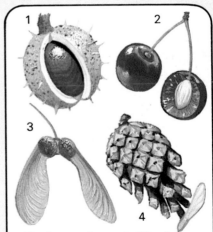

1

2

3

4

Fruits and seeds The horse chestnut (1), cherry (2) and sycamore 'aeroplane' (3) are all fruits and contain seeds. The pine cone (4) has seeds but is not a real fruit.

What to Record

There are several ways of studying trees. You can make collections of twigs and pressed leaves; you can press the flowers and collect the dried fruits and seeds; and you can make bark rubbings. All these activities will help you to identify the many different kinds of tree around you.

It is also interesting to keep a tree diary of one particular tree, or perhaps a few trees in your neighbourhood. Having identified your tree, try to work out how old it is. If it is growing in a park, the local council or the park-keeper may be able to tell you when it was planted. Alternatively, you can get some idea of the age from the girth of the trunk at a height of about 1.5 metres. Many common trees

How Old is a Tree? A tree forms a new ring of wood each year. When a tree is cut down you can find its age by counting the number of rings on the stump.

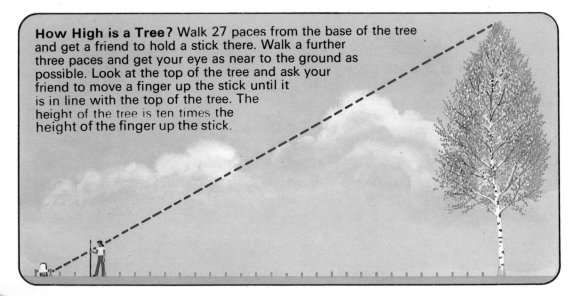

How High is a Tree? Walk 27 paces from the base of the tree and get a friend to hold a stick there. Walk a further three paces and get your eye as near to the ground as possible. Look at the top of the tree and ask your friend to move a finger up the stick until it is in line with the top of the tree. The height of the tree is ten times the height of the finger up the stick.

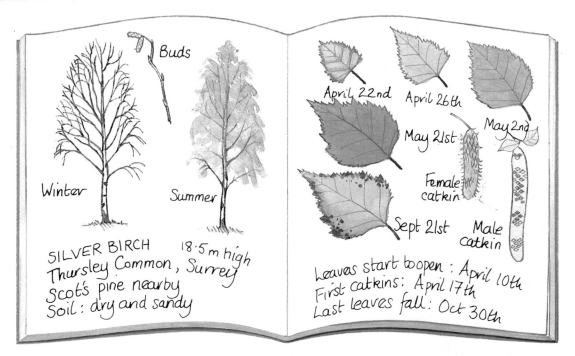

Buds

Winter   Summer

April 22nd   April 26th

May 21st   May 2nd

Female
catkin

Sept 21st   Male
catkin

SILVER BIRCH   18·5 m high
Thursley Common, Surrey
Scot's pine nearby
Soil: dry and sandy

Leaves start to open: April 10th
First catkins: April 17th
Last leaves fall: Oct 30th

▲ **A Tree Diary** Record the most important events which happen to your tree during the year. Make drawings of its shape and how fast the newly opened leaves grow or press the leaves and mount them. Say where it grows and give dates of when it flowers and loses its leaves.

▼ **Watch the Buds** In the Spring, if you cut a few twigs from a horse chestnut and put them in water, you can watch the sticky bud scales fold back to reveal the leaves. See how long the leaves take to unfold fully and notice which of the buds have flowers in them.

increase their girth by about 2.5cm per year when growing alone, and so a tree with a girth of 2.5 metres is likely to be about 100 years old. If it is growing in a wood, it will be more like 200 years old, because trees grow more slowly in woods.

If you estimate the height of your tree each year, you will be able to see how quickly it grows. Some trees add three metres in a year. You can also try to find out the different types of birds and animals which live in your tree or eat its fruits.

An Assortment of Leaves

With a little practice, it is possible to identify all the common trees from their leaves. The shape and texture of the leaves are the most important features: the size varies rather a lot. A typical leaf has a flat blade and a stalk, or petiole, although many leaves are stalkless. There is usually one main vein, called the mid-rib, with a number of smaller veins branching from it. The veins carry water and minerals to the leaves and take food away to other parts.

The edge of the leaf, or margin, is usually toothed and it may be deeply lobed. Sometimes the leaf surface is completely split into separate leaflets. Such leaves are called compound leaves. The leaflets may be in two rows along the mid-rib, or they may fan out from one point.

▼ **Holly** is an evergreen because it keeps its leaves throughout the winter. Its thick leathery leaves can withstand cold winter winds.

COMPOUND LEAVES

Common ash

Horse chestnut

Mimosa

Locust tree

Walnut

Tree of Heaven

LOBED LEAVES

Tulip tree

London plane

Field maple

Common oak

Hawtho

UNLOBED LEAVES

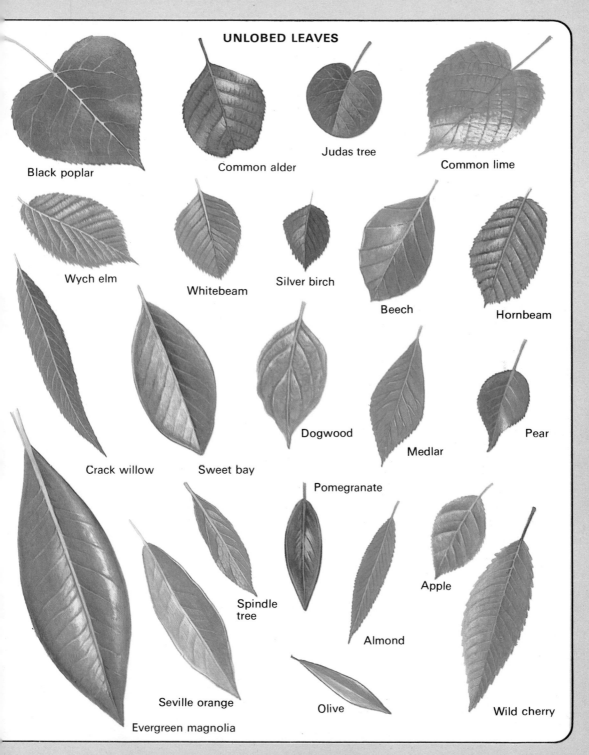

Black poplar

Common alder

Judas tree

Common lime

Wych elm

Whitebeam

Silver birch

Beech

Hornbeam

Crack willow

Sweet bay

Dogwood

Medlar

Pear

Pomegranate

Spindle tree

Almond

Apple

Seville orange

Olive

Wild cherry

Evergreen magnolia

A hover fly pollinating rowan flowers in early summer.

Whitebeam

Blackthorn

Flowers and Fruits

Apart from the conifers, or cone-bearers, all trees have flowers. The flowers are not always as obvious as the ones shown here, but they are extremely important: they produce the seeds from which new plants grow. Except for the mulberry and olive, all these trees rely on insects to carry pollen from flower to flower. These insects are attracted by the bright petals, the scent, and the nectar they come to feed on. The pollen enables the flower to make seeds which are always enclosed in fruits. Animals, especially birds, eat the soft fruits and so help scatter the seeds.

FRUITS

Whitebeam

Blackthorn

True service tree

Common pear

A blackbird eating rowan fruits.

True service tree

Common pear

Elder

Orange

Wild cherry

Mulberry

Elder

Orange

Wild cherry

Mulberry

Crab apple

Pomegranate

Olive

Crab apple

Pomegranate

Olive

Blowing in the Wind

Not all flowers need insects to carry their pollen. Some rely on the wind. They do not need bright colours or sweet scent. Most of them are small and dull.

Often the pollen is made in different flowers from the ones which produce the seeds. The male, or pollen-producing flowers, are usually grouped into long, swaying catkins. When the wind blows, the catkins move and scatter pollen. This drifts through the air until it reaches a female seed-producing flower and 'pollinates' it. Most wind-pollinated trees flower early in the year, before the leaves are fully open. The leaves do not then get in the way of the drifting pollen.

White poplar catkins (male) scatter pollen in the wind. The leaves of the white poplar (right) are white and downy underneath.

◀ **Lombardy poplar** relies on the wind to scatter its pollen.

▼ **Ash** flowers open early in the year and scatter pollen on the wind.

▼ **Elm** flowers appear long before the leaves. The wind scatters the pollen.

▼ **Aspen** catkins sway in the wind to scatter their pollen.

Lombardy poplar

Ash

Aspen

Elm

When pollen lands on a female flower it grows down into it and fertilises it. 'Egg-cells' in the female flower then begin to grow into seeds. At the same time, fruits swell up around the seeds. Those which are scattered by the wind have some kind of 'wing' on which they can drift through the air when they are ripe (right). By drifting away from the parent tree, the seeds have a better chance of growing up. They will not be crowded together competing for space, or overshadowed by their parent.

Poplar and willow trees scatter fluffy seeds. The other trees seen here release complete fruits.

Ash

Lime

Alder

Maple

Sycamore

Hornbeam

Smooth-leaved elm

Silver birch

▼ **Common lime** is pollinated by insects but its seeds are dispersed by the wind.

▼ **Crack willow** is insect-pollinated but its seeds are scattered by the wind.

▼ **Silver birch** catkins open with the leaves. Male catkins hang down, whereas the female catkins are upright.

▼ **Hornbeam** is pollinated by the wind and its seeds are wind-dispersed.

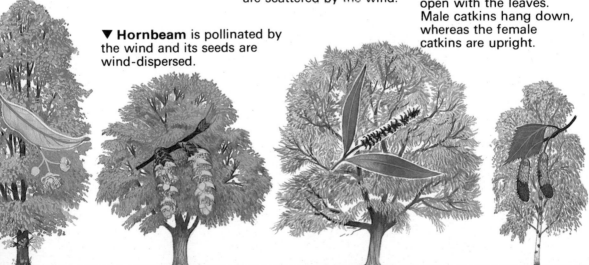

Common lime   **Hornbeam**   **Crack willow**   **Silver birch**

Woodland Fruits

Many woodland trees produce fruits with tough, woody coats after their flowers have been pollinated. These fruits are called nuts. Common examples include acorns, sweet chestnuts, beech nuts, and hazel nuts. Hazel nuts have particularly hard, thick shells.

If you crack open some of these nuts, you will see that each contains a single seed surrounded by its own thin coat. You usually remove this coat before you eat a sweet chestnut. The horse chestnut, or conker, which is not good to eat, is just a seed. It has only one coat which is much thinner than the shell of the sweet chestnut.

The seed inside a nut consists of a miniature plant and a store of food. Many birds and other animals find the food very tasty and they collect and eat a lot of nuts. They also bury some, and if they cannot find them again the seeds can grow into new trees.

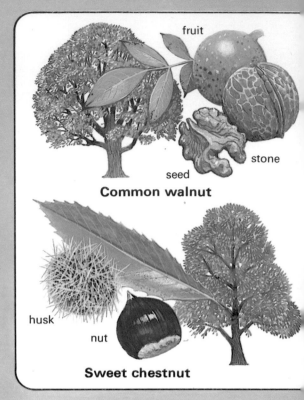

fruit

stone

seed

Common walnut

husk

nut

Sweet chestnut

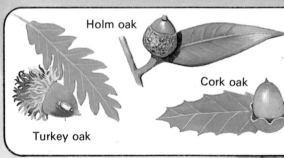

Holm oak

Cork oak

Turkey oak

▼ **Hazel nuts** Woodmice are very fond of hazel nuts and gather great stores of them for the winter. They gnaw through the hard shells easily with their sharp teeth.

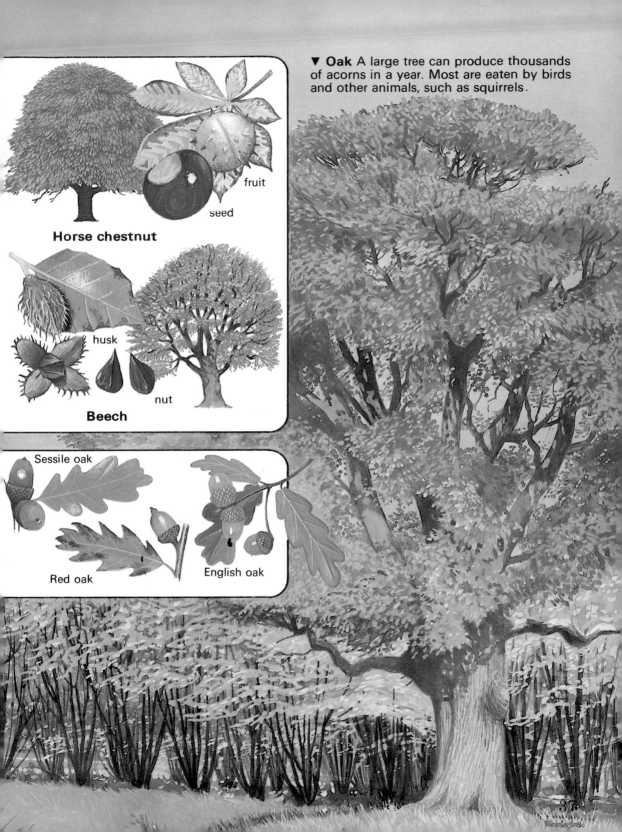

Horse chestnut

fruit

seed

Beech

husk

nut

Sessile oak

Red oak

English oak

▼ **Oak** A large tree can produce thousands of acorns in a year. Most are eaten by birds and other animals, such as squirrels.

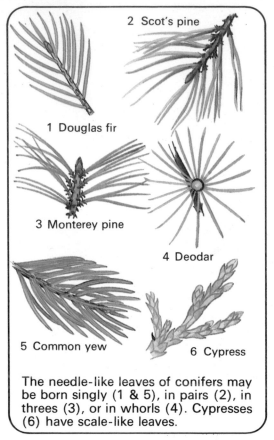

2 Scot's pine

1 Douglas fir

3 Monterey pine

4 Deodar

5 Common yew

6 Cypress

The needle-like leaves of conifers may be born singly (1 & 5), in pairs (2), in threes (3), or in whorls (4). Cypresses (6) have scale-like leaves.

Conifers

Conifers have no real flowers or fruits. You find their seeds in woody cones. The conifers you will see most often are pines, firs, cedars, spruces (which are used as Christmas trees), and larches. Larches are unusual because they are deciduous which means that they lose their leaves for the winter. Almost all other conifers are evergreens.

The small reddish female cones begin life in spring, often right at the tips of the branches. At the same time, clusters of little male cones develop. These are yellowish and they scatter clouds of pollen. The wind carries the pollen to the open female cones. Having been pollinated, the female cones close up and swell as the seeds grow inside. The cones become green and then, when the seeds are ripe, brown and woody. Then they open again and release their seeds to the wind. The whole process may take just a few months or as much as two years. The yew is not a true conifer; its seeds form in individual fleshy cups instead of cones.

female flower

seed

mature female cones

▲ **Sitka Spruce** Many conifers come from cold lands. Their sloping branches shed the snow easily. Although the trees are evergreen, the leaves do not last for ever. Some fall each year. Spruce leaves grow on little woody pegs. Birds, like this crossbill, like to eat its seeds.

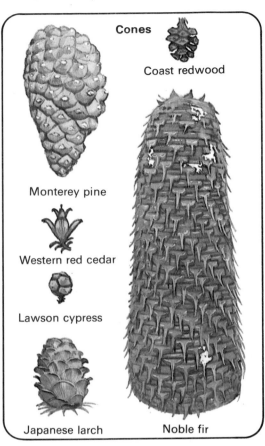

Cones

Coast redwood

Monterey pine

Western red cedar

Lawson cypress

Japanese larch

Noble fir

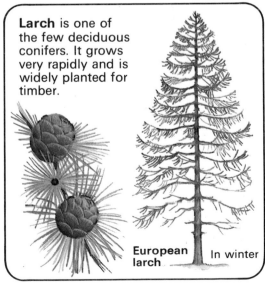

Larch is one of the few deciduous conifers. It grows very rapidly and is widely planted for timber.

European larch

In winter

Silver fir

Western
hemlock

Douglas fir

Wellingtonia

Coast redwood

Conifers can survive under very harsh conditions – high up on cold and windy mountains, or in hot dry areas where there is little water. This is because their needle-like leaves are tough and leathery and so do not lose much water.

The two largest kinds of tree in the world are both conifers. The coast redwood has been known to grow as tall as 112 metres, while the Wellingtonia, or 'big tree', though not as tall, has a massive trunk. Some are estimated to have lived for well over 3000 years.

Grand fir

Scot's pine

Corsican pine

Yew

Stone pine

Aleppo pine

Juniper cones have fleshy scales which make them more like berries. Cypress cones are also round but they are woody. Junipers, cypresses, and the western red cedar are often planted in parks and gardens for their beauty.

Juniper

Italian cypress

Western red cedar

Lawson cypress

Juniper cones

Italian Cypress cone

41

Parks and Gardens

Some of the most beautiful trees are most often seen only in parks and gardens because they do not grow naturally wild in Britain. The monkey puzzle's stiff spiky-looking branches make it a most attractive ornamental tree. The cedar of Lebanon, with its spreading 'skirts' of dark foliage, dramatically adorns the lawns of large country houses. Some trees combine beauty with an ability to withstand the polluted air of city streets.

Ginkgo or maidenhair Comes from China but is probably extinct in the wild. It is a relative of the conifers.

▶ **Cedar of Lebanon**
A very wide tree with almost horizontal branches and upright cones which take two or three years to ripen.

Cedar of Lebanon

Monkey puzzle Also known as the Chile pine, it comes originally from the Andes. Its tough, triangular leaves are very sharp.

London plane

▲ **London plane** This is frequently grown in towns because it can survive well in a polluted atmosphere. It is easily recognised by its bark which flakes off leaving yellowish patches.

Canary palm

Chusan palm

▲ **Palms** are attractive flowering trees found mainly in the tropics. Among many species are the date, oil, and coconut palms. The Chusan and Canary palms seen here are widely grown for ornament.

Judas tree

Laburnum

Campbell's magnolia

▲ Three of the most beautiful flowering trees that grow in our gardens: the magnolia comes from the Himalayas; the Judas tree and laburnum both come from Southern Europe.

43

Below, starting top left: Limpet, cowrie, auger, olive shell, volute, chank shell, cat's-eye shell, scallop, tusk shell and conch.

SHELLS

The hobby of shell-collecting is an easy one to start, and can make your seaside holiday even greater fun. Shells are not hard to find, and they are easy to keep once you have cleaned them. People study shells throughout the world, but you really need go no further than your nearest beach to make a start on your collection. The scientific study of shells is called 'conchology'.

The next few pages show some of the different kinds of shells that are found in the world's seas. There are shells from sandy, rocky and muddy beaches, and extraordinary, rare and exotic shells. You will also find out exactly what shells are, and how they are formed.

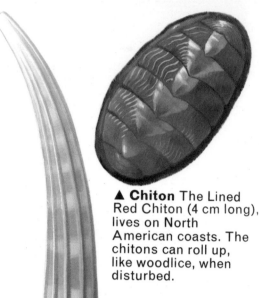

▲ **Chiton** The Lined
Red Chiton (4 cm long),
lives on North
American coasts. The
chitons can roll up,
like woodlice, when
disturbed.

◀ **Tusk shells,** like
this one, *Dentalium
vernedi*, from Japan,
burrow in sand. It is
9 cm long, but most
tusk shells are small
and difficult to name.

▲ **Nautilus** The beautiful
Pearly Nautilus (20 cm wide)
swims in tropical waters. It is
related to octopuses, squids
and cuttlefishes.

What are Seashells?

Seashells are skeletons. Humans have skeletons inside their bodies, called internal skeletons, but many animals have skeletons outside their bodies. Shells are the hard outer coverings of animals which we call molluscs. Insects, crabs and sea urchins also have outer skeletons, and it is important not to mistake their skeletons for seashells.

The shells protect the molluscs' soft bodies from other animals and from the waves. Most molluscs live in the sea but some live on land and a few in fresh water.

The five major groups of molluscs are pictured on these two pages. There is also a sixth group which was only discovered in 1950. These rare cap-shaped shells are called *Neopilina*. It is unlikely that you will find any of these shells because they live in very deep waters.

The most common group of molluscs are the *gastropods*. Most gastropods have a single shell. This may be coiled, as in winkles and whelks, or dome-shaped as in limpets. The two-part shells, or *bivalves*, are the next largest group.

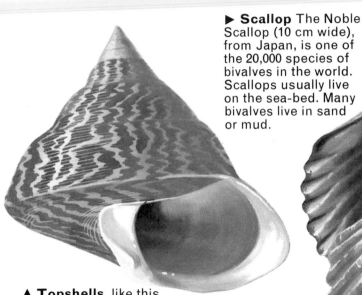

▶ **Scallop** The Noble Scallop (10 cm wide), from Japan, is one of the 20,000 species of bivalves in the world. Scallops usually live on the sea-bed. Many bivalves live in sand or mud.

▲ **Topshells**, like this *Calliostoma tigris* (5 cm high), from New Zealand, are gastropods. There are about 80,000 types of gastropods in the world. Many are found on rocks or stones.

The next three groups are not as common. Chitons, or coat-of-mail shells, are made up of eight separate plates. A few types of chitons have been found in deep water, but most are found on rocks close to the shore. Most tusk shells – shaped like the tusks of an elephant – also live in shallow waters. *Cephalopods* include the Nautilus, octopus, squid and cuttlefish. Of these, only the Nautilus has an outer shell. It lives in tropical waters and is quite rare. You are not likely to find it on your local beach. However, the 'bones' of its relative, the cuttlefish, can often be found on beaches all around the world.

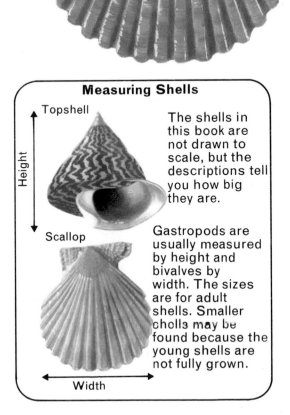

Measuring Shells

Topshell

Height

Scallop

Width

The shells in this book are not drawn to scale, but the descriptions tell you how big they are.

Gastropods are usually measured by height and bivalves by width. The sizes are for adult shells. Smaller shells may be found because the young shells are not fully grown.

47

How Shells are Made

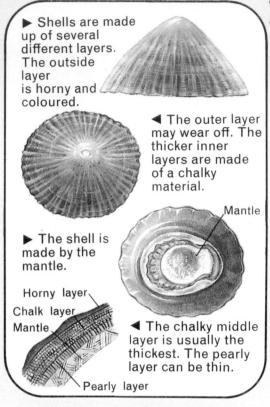

▶ Shells are made up of several different layers. The outside layer is horny and coloured.

◀ The outer layer may wear off. The thicker inner layers are made of a chalky material.

▶ The shell is made by the mantle.

Mantle

Horny layer
Chalk layer
Mantle

◀ The chalky middle layer is usually the thickest. The pearly layer can be thin.

Pearly layer

Molluscs grow shells rather as humans grow nails. The shell is produced by a fold of skin called the *mantle* and is built up in layers from it. The layers harden and are dead, just as the ends of nails are dead. Shell is made of a mixture of horn and chalky crystals which remains after the mollusc dies. The mollusc is attached to its shell by muscles.

The shell grows with the animal. The little whorls at the end of a Nautilus or winkle shell were made when the molluscs were tiny. Shells grow quickly when there is plenty of food and the water is warm. In cold water the shell grows slowly. The different growth rates cause ridges on the shell.

▼ **Bivalve shells**, like the Quahog, are usually joined at the hinge, or beak. There are teeth in the hinge. Sometimes it is possible to see the scars left by the muscles that held the shells shut. The Quahog has ridges across its shell. Some shells have ribs coming from the hinge.

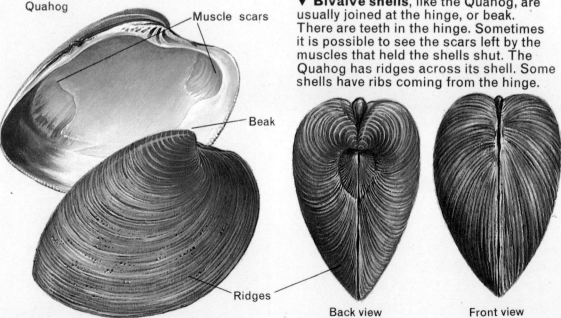

Quahog

Muscle scars

Beak

Ridges

Back view

Front view

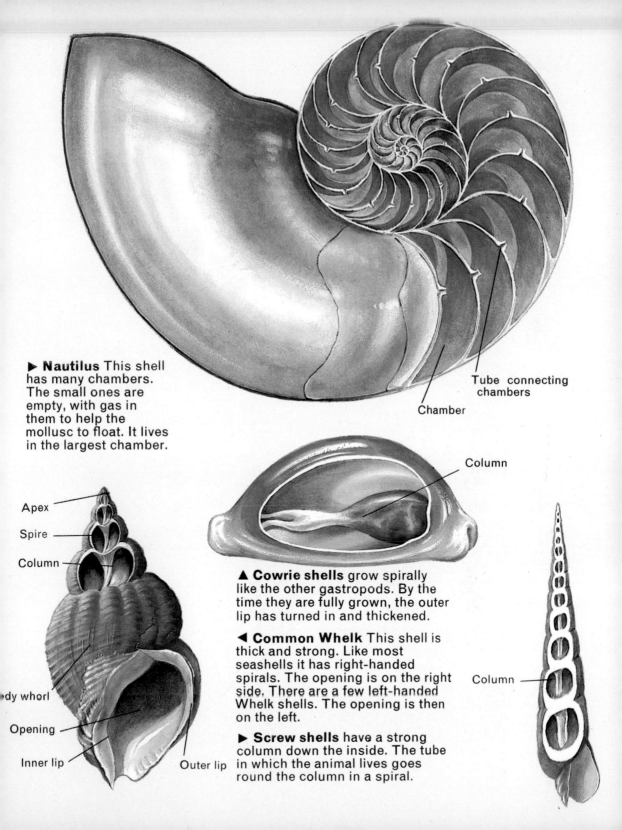

▶ **Nautilus** This shell has many chambers. The small ones are empty, with gas in them to help the mollusc to float. It lives in the largest chamber.

Tube connecting chambers

Chamber

Column

Apex

Spire

Column

dy whorl

Opening

Inner lip

Outer lip

▲ **Cowrie shells** grow spirally like the other gastropods. By the time they are fully grown, the outer lip has turned in and thickened.

◀ **Common Whelk** This shell is thick and strong. Like most seashells it has right-handed spirals. The opening is on the right side. There are a few left-handed Whelk shells. The opening is then on the left.

▶ **Screw shells** have a strong column down the inside. The tube in which the animal lives goes round the column in a spiral.

Column

What to Look For

Most of the shells you will find belong to the two main groups of shells – bivalves and gastropods. Some of the bivalves are shown below. Although these shells are in pairs when the mollusc is alive, the hinge usually breaks when it dies. So you will often only find one shell.

Some gastropod shells have a very simple form. Limpets are a flattened-cone shape. Slipper limpets are a little more complicated, with a small shelf on the inside. Some shells, like the ormers or abalones, have a line of holes along the top. The rest of the gastropods are much more complicated, with shells twisted into *whorls*. Some, like the winkles, have only a few whorls. Others, like the tower shells, have as many as 14.

Most gastropods have right-handed or *dextral* whorls, with the opening on the right. A few have openings on the left, with left-handed or *sinistral* whorls. These are much sought after by collectors.

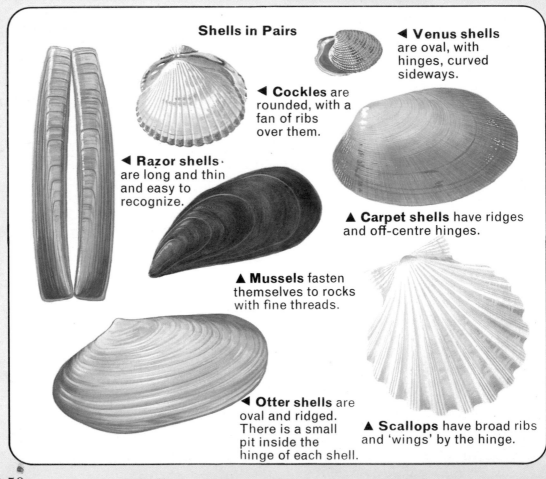

Shells in Pairs

◀ **Venus shells** are oval, with hinges, curved sideways.

◀ **Cockles** are rounded, with a fan of ribs over them.

◀ **Razor shells** are long and thin and easy to recognize.

▲ **Carpet shells** have ridges and off-centre hinges.

▲ **Mussels** fasten themselves to rocks with fine threads.

◀ **Otter shells** are oval and ridged. There is a small pit inside the hinge of each shell.

▲ **Scallops** have broad ribs and 'wings' by the hinge.

Common Limpet

White Tortoiseshell Limpet

◄ **Limpets** are single shells that look like cones. They have no whorls, the shell sits over the animal like a hat.

◄ **Ormers** or abalones are shells with a long row of holes in them. They live on rocks and are not found in cold waters.

Ormer

► **Cowrie shells** are usually very shiny and smooth. The thin openings are almost as long as the shell.

European Cowrie

► **Slipper Limpets** have a small shelf to protect the animal. They may be found in chains of up to 12.

Slipper Limpet

Chain living Slipper Limpets

◄ **Topshells and periwinkles** are cone-shaped, but with whorls. Periwinkles are more rounded than topshells and some are very small.

Periwinkle

Topshell

Common Whelk

1   1   1   1

15   12   14   7

Needle Shell   Wentletrap   Tower Shell   Spire Shell

▲ **Tall, pointed shells** The number of whorls on these shells helps to tell which is which. Some have thicker ridges or ribs. Colours do not help as they vary from shell to shell.

▲ **Whelks** have thick heavy shells with ridges on them, and also a lip.

51

Collecting Shells

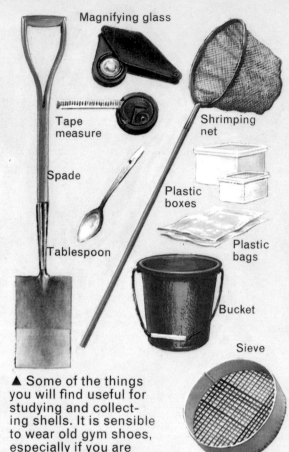

Magnifying glass

Tape measure

Spade

Tablespoon

Shrimping net

Plastic boxes

Plastic bags

Bucket

Sieve

▲ Some of the things you will find useful for studying and collecting shells. It is sensible to wear old gym shoes, especially if you are looking on a rocky beach.

The best time for studying and collecting shells is at low tide, when the beaches are not covered by the sea. When you are exploring a beach, keep an eye on the time to make sure that you are not going to be cut off when the sea comes in. The equipment pictured left will be useful. But the most important thing to take with you is a notebook and pencil to record the type of shell you find.

On a sandy shore you can often find empty shells on the strand line – or high-tide mark. You will not find live molluscs here because it is too dry for them.

To study live molluscs on sandy or muddy shores, you will need to dig deeply with a spade at the low-tide mark. Fill a sieve with the sand

Keeping a Record

Name: Topshell
Date found: 1st July 79
Where found: In sea-weed on rocks.
Description:

2.5 cm

You should make full notes of all the shells you find. The notebook (left) shows you the sort of notes you should make. It is also useful to draw a picture of the shell. You can then put all your notes and drawings into a scrapbook (above) so that you have a record of all your findings.

or mud and wash it away. You may then find some bivalves left in the sieve. Take notes, and replace them. You can watch them digging back into the sand with their *foot*.

Studying molluscs is easier on a rocky shore because the animals cannot dig themselves in. Molluscs can be found sheltering under seaweed or in cracks and under rocks. A shrimping net is useful for exploring rock pools. Some molluscs live right at the top of a rocky beach in the upper shore. If you move rocks or stones to look under them, remember to replace them carefully. Be gentle too with the molluscs and put them back where you found them.

Empty shells can be washed in fresh water and brushed with a soft brush. They are then ready to be recorded and stored.

Where to Look

▲ **Sandy shores** are good places to look for shells, especially when the tide is out. You will find mostly bivalve shells.

▲ **Rocky shores** have many different kinds of shells clinging to the rocks. Look in crevices and cracks, and in pools.

▲ **Muddy shores** Low tide is the best time to search muddy shores and estuaries.

Storing Shells

Rubber band
Plastic
Label
Matchbox

Once the shells have been washed and carefully dried they can be stored in boxes. Line the box with cotton wool and stretch plastic film over it to keep out dust. You can use matchboxes and margarine cartons. Each box should have the name of the shell and the location marked on the outside.

Plastic filing box

Shells on Sandy Beaches

Most of the shells found on sandy beaches are bivalves. The live molluscs are buried in the damp sand, away from the heat of the sun. They come up to the surface to feed when the tide comes in.

In deeper waters the molluscs do not have to burrow, because the tide does not uncover them. It is more difficult to collect shells from deeper waters. You will usually have to wait for the sea to wash them ashore. Some of the deeper water shells move about on the sea-bed quite quickly by shooting water from a tube called a *siphon*.

Some of the shells that can be found on sandy beaches are shown on these two pages. It is unlikely that all these shells will be found, and you may find some that are not illustrated here.

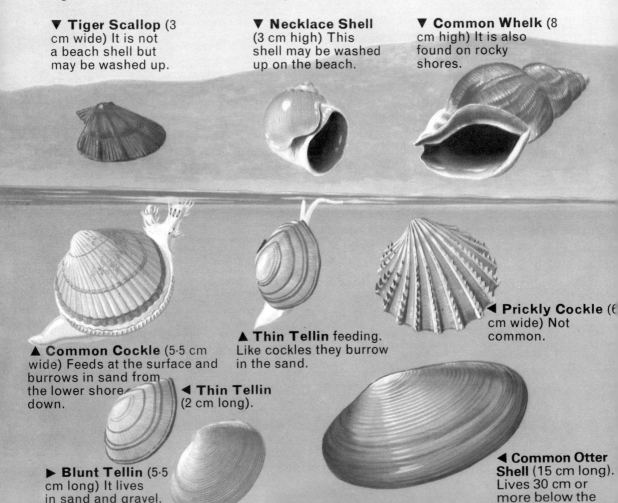

▼ **Tiger Scallop** (3 cm wide) It is not a beach shell but may be washed up.

▼ **Necklace Shell** (3 cm high) This shell may be washed up on the beach.

▼ **Common Whelk** (8 cm high) It is also found on rocky shores.

◄ **Prickly Cockle** (6 cm wide) Not common.

▲ **Common Cockle** (5·5 cm wide) Feeds at the surface and burrows in sand from the lower shore down.

▲ **Thin Tellin** feeding. Like cockles they burrow in the sand.

◄ **Thin Tellin** (2 cm long).

► **Blunt Tellin** (5·5 cm long) It lives in sand and gravel.

◄ **Common Otter Shell** (15 cm long). Lives 30 cm or more below the surface.

Tides and Zones

Twice a day, the beaches are washed by the tides. Twice a month, when the moon is full or new, these tides rise very high and fall very low. These are the spring tides. Twice a month, when the moon is half full, the tides do not move up and down as far. These are the neap tides. The differences in the tides make zones on the beach.

The splash zone, at the top of the beach, is only covered by water at the highest spring tides. The upper-shore zone is the area between the high-water lines of the spring and neap tides. The lower shore is the area between the low-water lines of the spring and neap tides. The area in between is the middle shore.

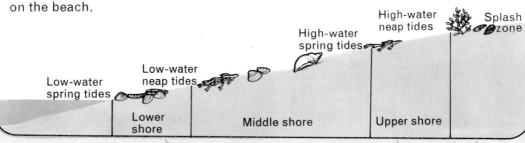

High-water neap tides

Splash zone

High-water spring tides

Low-water neap tides

Low-water spring tides

Lower shore

Middle shore

Upper shore

▶ **Dog Cockle** (6 cm wide) Burrows just below the surface and is often washed ashore.

▶ **Queen Scallop** (5-7·5 cm wide) It lives just below low tide mark.

◀ **Pelican's Foot** Shell (5 cm high) It is found on muddy gravel and on sand.

▼ **Rayed Artemis** (5 cm wide) Found in sandy bays on the lower shore and below.

▲ **Striped Venus** (3 cm wide) lives in the lower shore zone.

▲ **Banded Venus** (2·5 cm wide) It lives in the middle shore zone down to the sea.

▲ **Banded Wedge Shell** (3 cm long) It lives in the middle and lower zones of exposed shores.

▶ **Small Razor Shell** (10 cm long).

▲ **Rayed Trough** (5 cm wide) Usually lives just offshore.

◀ **Sand Gaper** (12 cm long) The two halves of the shell gape when closed.

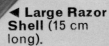

◀ **Large Razor Shell** (15 cm long).

Rocky Shores

Most of the shells found on rocky shores are gastropods. The molluscs crawl over the surface of the rocks, scraping off the greenish film of algae or browsing on different kinds of seaweed. They scrape at food with their rough tongues. When the tide goes out, they clamp down onto the rock to keep in their body moisture.

Shells on rocky shores are exposed to the beating of the waves when the sea is rough, and they have to be able to stand up to the battering. Limpets can survive in very rough conditions, and they can be found everywhere. The molluscs which cannot grip the rock tightly will only be found in crevices on exposed shores.

Rock and Wood Borers

Common Piddock (9 cm long)

Oval Piddock (6 cm long)

Flask Shell (3 cm long)

Shipworm (up to 30 cm long)

Not all molluscs burrow into sand. A few bore into rocks and wood. The Shipworm bores into wood and causes a lot of damage to boats and piers. The Common Piddock is also found in wood, but it usually burrows in chalk or sandstone. The Oval Piddock is found in shale and clay. Flask Shells bore into sandstone or limestone.

▼ **Painted Topshell** (2·5 cm high) It is pearly under the coloured horny layer.

▼ **Edible Periwinkles** (2·5 cm high) are a common species on the lower shore.

▼ **Needle Shell** (1·2 cm high) It is found among stones and debris.

▶ **Keyhole Limpet** (1·5 cm high) It lives on lower shore rocks.

◀ **Chinaman's Hat** (2 cm high) It clamps on stones and other shells.

▶ **Common Wentletrap** (3·5 cm high) It has ribs that stand out and is found on the lower shore.

▶ **European Cowries** (4 cm long) are small and ribbed.

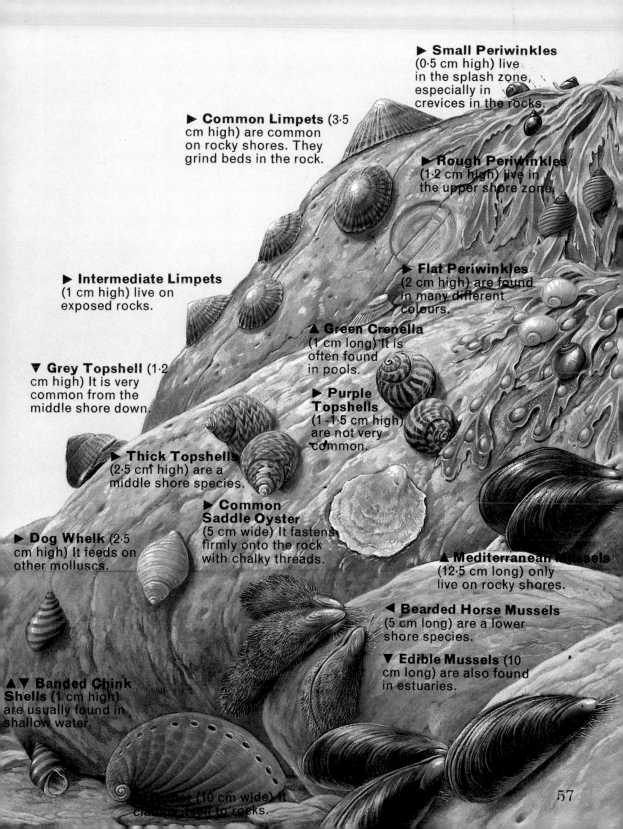

► **Small Periwinkles** (0·5 cm high) live in the splash zone, especially in crevices in the rocks.

► **Common Limpets** (3·5 cm high) are common on rocky shores. They grind beds in the rock.

► **Rough Periwinkles** (1·2 cm high) live in the upper shore zone.

► **Intermediate Limpets** (1 cm high) live on exposed rocks.

► **Flat Periwinkles** (2 cm high) are found in many different colours.

▲ **Green Crenella** (1 cm long) It is often found in pools.

▼ **Grey Topshell** (1·2 cm high) It is very common from the middle shore down.

► **Purple Topshells** (1 - 1·5 cm high) are not very common.

► **Thick Topshells** (2·5 cm high) are a middle shore species.

► **Common Saddle Oyster** (5 cm wide) It fastens firmly onto the rock with chalky threads.

► **Dog Whelk** (2·5 cm high) It feeds on other molluscs.

▲ **Mediterranean Mussels** (12·5 cm long) only live on rocky shores.

◄ **Bearded Horse Mussels** (5 cm long) are a lower shore species.

▼ **Edible Mussels** (10 cm long) are also found in estuaries.

▲▼ **Banded Chink Shells** (1 cm high) are usually found in shallow water.

(10 cm wide) It clamps itself to rocks.

Estuaries and Muddy Shores

Estuaries are found where rivers run into the sea. Rivers carry soil which is deposited in the estuaries, making the shores muddy. These shores are washed by salt water when the tide is in, and by fresh water from the river when the tide is out. This makes an estuary a difficult place to live in.

There are, however, some advantages to life in an estuary. The river brings down plenty of food, so that these areas are quite well populated. As on a sandy shore, there are many bivalves. Some of them burrow in the mud. Others, such as mussels and oysters, grow on rocks or piers, fastened by short threads.

Apart from the seashells, there may be shells of freshwater molluscs which have been washed down stream. These freshwater shells are usually much thinner than seashells.

In the tropics, the estuaries often spread out into mangrove swamps. Many colourful molluscs are found there. Some are cemented to the roots of the mangrove trees and others crawl about on them, above the mud. The combination of warmth and plenty of food produces a large population of molluscs.

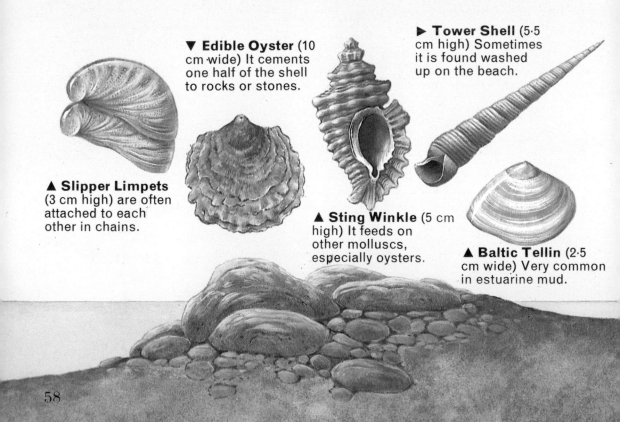

▼ **Edible Oyster** (10 cm wide) It cements one half of the shell to rocks or stones.

▶ **Tower Shell** (5·5 cm high) Sometimes it is found washed up on the beach.

▲ **Slipper Limpets** (3 cm high) are often attached to each other in chains.

▲ **Sting Winkle** (5 cm high) It feeds on other molluscs, especially oysters.

▲ **Baltic Tellin** (2·5 cm wide) Very common in estuarine mud.

Shells from Mangrove Swamps

Mangrove Cerith
(4 cm high)

Telescope Shell (9 cm high)

Bleeding Tooth Nerite
(2 cm high)

Mangrove Tellin
(8 cm long)

Rough Winkle
(2 cm high)

Mud Creeper
(8–12 cm high)

American Crown Conch
(10 cm high)

West Indian Crown Conch
(10 cm high)

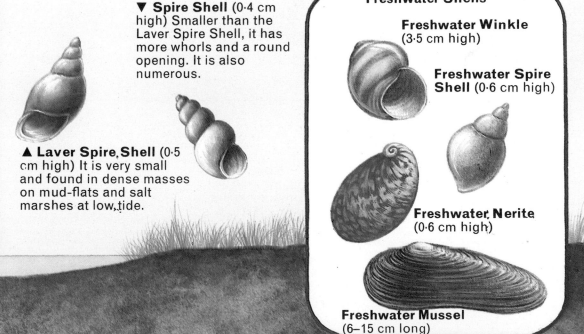

▼ **Spire Shell** (0·4 cm high) Smaller than the Laver Spire Shell, it has more whorls and a round opening. It is also numerous.

▲ **Laver Spire Shell** (0·5 cm high) It is very small and found in dense masses on mud-flats and salt marshes at low tide.

Freshwater Shells

Freshwater Winkle
(3·5 cm high)

Freshwater Spire Shell (0·6 cm high)

Freshwater Nerite
(0·6 cm high)

Freshwater Mussel
(6–15 cm long)

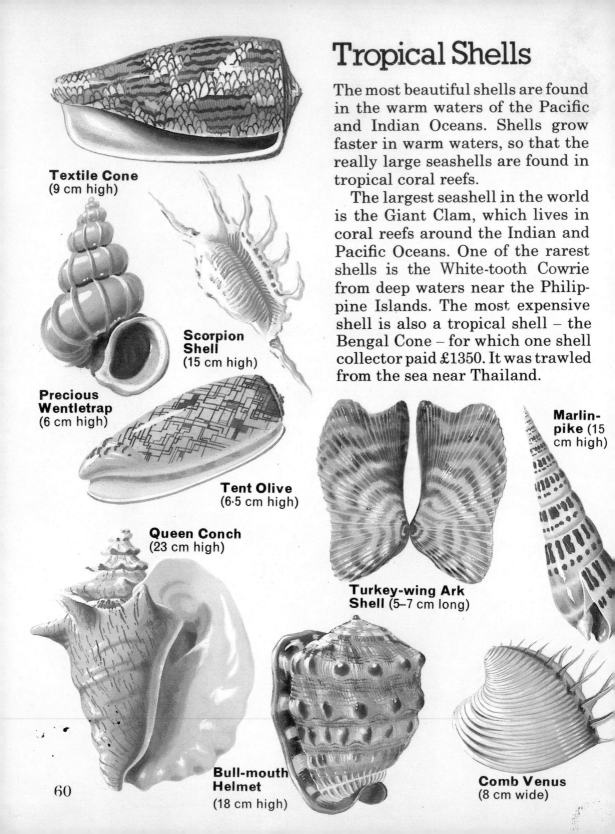

Textile Cone
(9 cm high)

Scorpion Shell
(15 cm high)

Precious Wentletrap
(6 cm high)

Tent Olive
(6·5 cm high)

Queen Conch
(23 cm high)

Turkey-wing Ark Shell (5–7 cm long)

Marlin-pike (15 cm high)

Bull-mouth Helmet
(18 cm high)

Comb Venus
(8 cm wide)

Tropical Shells

The most beautiful shells are found in the warm waters of the Pacific and Indian Oceans. Shells grow faster in warm waters, so that the really large seashells are found in tropical coral reefs.

The largest seashell in the world is the Giant Clam, which lives in coral reefs around the Indian and Pacific Oceans. One of the rarest shells is the White-tooth Cowrie from deep waters near the Philippine Islands. The most expensive shell is also a tropical shell – the Bengal Cone – for which one shell collector paid £1350. It was trawled from the sea near Thailand.

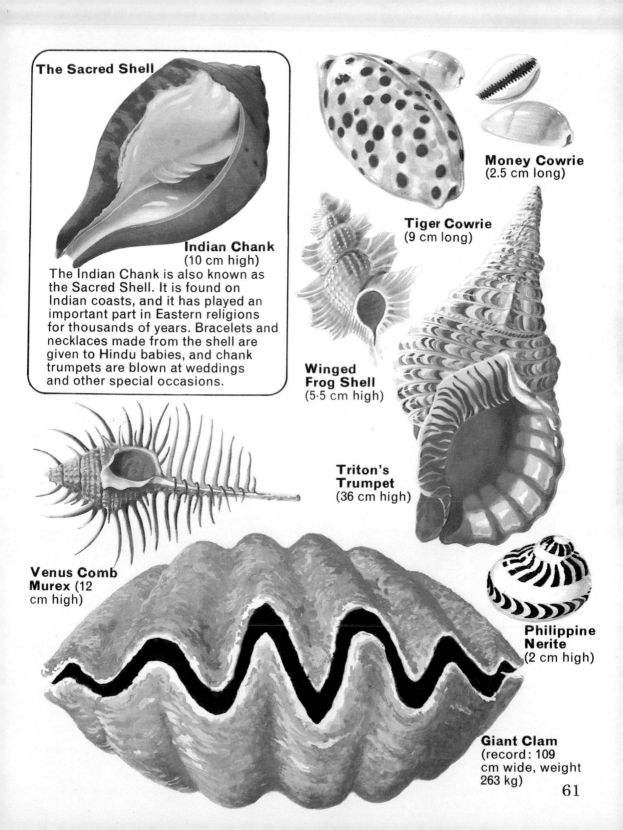

The Sacred Shell

Indian Chank
(10 cm high)

The Indian Chank is also known as the Sacred Shell. It is found on Indian coasts, and it has played an important part in Eastern religions for thousands of years. Bracelets and necklaces made from the shell are given to Hindu babies, and chank trumpets are blown at weddings and other special occasions.

Money Cowrie
(2.5 cm long)

Tiger Cowrie
(9 cm long)

Winged Frog Shell
(5·5 cm high)

Triton's Trumpet
(36 cm high)

Venus Comb Murex (12 cm high)

Philippine Nerite
(2 cm high)

Giant Clam
(record: 109 cm wide, weight 263 kg)

61

▼ **Cameos** are carved from shells, such as this Black Helmet Shell which lives in warm Mediterranean waters.

▲ **Byssus cloth** is made from the long silk-like threads of the Noble Pen Shell. The cloth was made into gloves and other garments.

▼ **Mother-of-pearl** is ma from the inside layer of many shells. These butto were made from the Green Abalone.

Using Shells

Shells have many uses. Large tropical shells, like the False Trumpet, have been used for carrying water. Small Indian Chanks were used as babies' feeding bottles in India.

Some shells have been used as money. The Money Cowrie was so named because it was used as a coin in many parts of the world. The Quahog was cut into beads by the North American Indians. The beads, called wampum, were used like money.

A few bivalves fasten themselves to rocks with threads called byssus.

Some of these threads are fine and silky and were used to weave fine cloth, rather like silk. The Noble Pen Shell, found in the Mediterranean Sea, was harvested in large numbers for its byssus.

Some molluscs have been valuable for the dye they produce. Two types of Mediterranean Murex produce a rich purple dye, called the Royal Purple. It was used to colour the borders on Roman senators' robes.

People have used shells as decoration and ornaments for thousands of years. Bracelets, necklaces and buttons have all been made from shells.

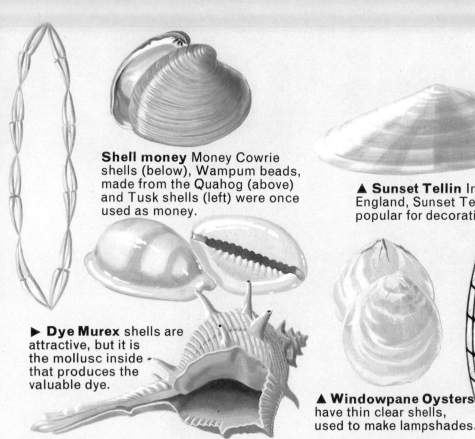

Shell money Money Cowrie shells (below), Wampum beads, made from the Quahog (above) and Tusk shells (left) were once used as money.

▲ **Sunset Tellin** In Victorian England, Sunset Tellins were popular for decoration.

▶ **Dye Murex** shells are attractive, but it is the mollusc inside that produces the valuable dye.

▲ **Windowpane Oysters** have thin clear shells, used to make lampshades.

Pearls, too, come from shells. The best pearls are produced by the Pearl Oyster, which lives in tropical waters. At one time Britain was famous for its freshwater pearls. The pearl is made when a tiny piece of grit irritates the soft tissue of the mollusc's mantle. The animal covers it with shell lining to protect itself, and this forms into a pearl.

Cameos are carved out of seashells. They are often made from helmet shells. The layers of these shells are different colours. The jeweller carves a design in the white layer and cuts around it down to the coloured layer.

Precious Pearls

In the past, the hundreds of Pearl Oysters, brought up from the seabed by Japanese divers gave just a few pearls. Today, there are Pearl Oyster farms in the warm waters around Japan. A bead is put into the oyster to start the pearl.

Below, from left to right: Long-eared owl, wood pigeon, blue tit, bullfinch and green woodpecker.

64

BIRDS

Birds are among the most attractive of all wild creatures. Many have lovely colours, and they walk, hop, fly, and nest in all sorts of interesting ways. They are also the easiest of all animals to see. While many wild mammals hide away, birds show themselves off to us, as they fly through the air or wander over the ground.

Birdwatching is an interesting hobby that you can start right away without any special equipment. The following pages should help you identify many of the birds you will see in different places. You will also find out what different birds are doing, and why they behave in the ways they do.

What to Look For

▲ The parts of a bird's body. This is a male redstart.

It is not difficult to find out the name of any bird that you see. Every kind of bird has something about it that no other kind has. Once you have learned these special features, you should be able to recognize most birds.

It helps to go birdwatching with people who know a lot about birds. They can point out the things you must look for. You should always take a field guide with you. This is a book with pictures of all the birds that you are likely to find in your region.

The first thing to look for when naming a bird is its size. A bird is measured from the tip of its beak to the tip of its tail. Birds of the same kind are always the same size. You would not see a big wren or a small crow, for example.

Shapes in Flight
Every bird has a certain way of flying. Recognizing this, and the outline of a bird, will help to identify it.

Tern

House Sparrow

Marsh Harrier

Pheasant

Different Colours

▲ Many birds, such as the turnstone, have one pattern of colours in summer (right) and another in winter (left).

▲ In some birds, like the goldfinch, the young birds (left) have a different pattern of colours from the adult birds (right).

▲ In many kinds of birds, such as mallard ducks, the male (right) and female (left) have different colours.

All Kinds of Beaks

Most birds use their beaks or bills to get food as well as to eat it. Every kind of bird has a certain type of beak that enables it to eat a particular range of food. The shape and size depends on the kind of food it eats, which in turn depends on where the bird lives. These are the beaks of several common kinds of birds.

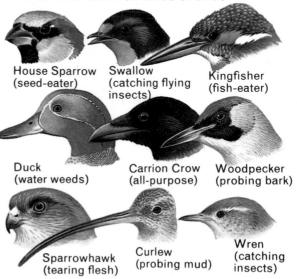

House Sparrow (seed-eater) Swallow (catching flying insects) Kingfisher (fish-eater)

Duck (water weeds) Carrion Crow (all-purpose) Woodpecker (probing bark)

Sparrowhawk (tearing flesh) Curlew (probing mud) Wren (catching insects)

The pattern of the colours in a bird's plumage is very important in finding its name. Most birds have their own particular colours. You only have to recognize the pattern and you will be able to identify the bird. However, some birds have similar patterns and you must then look for some other special feature.

The next thing to look at is the bird's body. Look for differences between beaks, feet and wing shapes. It is often hard to see a bird's colours when it is flying or in dim light. In these cases, you may have to rely on its body features to identify it.

You can also tell a bird by its song. The best way to learn bird songs is with an experienced bird-watcher. You can also learn them from records.

Crow   Jay   Hawk
Goose   Heron   Swift   Woodpecker

How and Where to Look

Wherever you look outdoors, you are likely to find birds. However, you will not see all the birds that live in a region by staying in one place. Different places have different kinds of birds, depending on the variety of food and nesting sites that each place has to offer. To see the different types of birds you will have to make special trips to the various *habitats* in which they make their homes.

There are good ways and bad ways to look for birds. It is important not to disturb any birds you find, in order to watch them behaving naturally. You must not take any eggs or harm young birds. You should also show consideration for people as well, for example, by closing farm gates.

If you follow a few simple rules, you will be able to get a lot of pleasure from birdwatching.

Always carry a notebook for sketching and making notes of the birds you see. You can also take a field guide to identify any new birds.

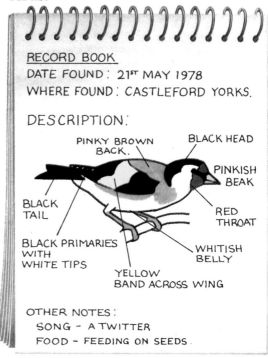

RECORD BOOK
DATE FOUND : 21ST MAY 1978
WHERE FOUND : CASTLEFORD YORKS.

DESCRIPTION :

PINKY BROWN BACK.
BLACK HEAD
PINKISH BEAK
BLACK TAIL
RED THROAT
BLACK PRIMARIES WITH WHITE TIPS
WHITISH BELLY
YELLOW BAND ACROSS WING

OTHER NOTES :
SONG - A TWITTER
FOOD - FEEDING ON SEEDS.

▲ You should make a full description of the birds you see, especially any new ones or birds you do not recognize. The notebook shows the notes you would make on seeing a goldfinch (left).

How to Draw Birds

First draw an oval for the head and one for the body. Join the shapes together and add the eye, beak, tail and legs.

Now add the wing shape. Complete the picture by smoothing the shape with a dark line and putting in the feathers.

Draw the two ovals for the head and body as before. Join them together and add the beak and tail.

Now draw in the eye. By following the above diagram, draw in the wings. Finish off as before.

A duck can be drawn by making the two ovals, leaving enough room for the longer neck. Join up the shapes and put in the eye and tail.

Now draw in the wing and leg. Finish off as before.
A perching bird (right) can be drawn by making its toes curl around a branch.

You may need to use binoculars to look at birds more closely. Always keep the strap of the binoculars around your neck, so that you do not drop them. Try to wear dull-coloured clothes so that the birds will not easily spot you. If possible, use trees, bushes, hedges and walls to conceal yourself. To get very close to birds, you may have to put up a *hide* and wait patiently inside.

Habitats and Reserves

The main kinds of bird habitats and the birds that live in them are shown on the following pages. The birds that you can see in each habitat will depend on the time of year.

You can also see interesting birds at reserves. These are protected places where birds come to live. You will need permission or have to pay admission to enter.

Birds of Ponds and Streams

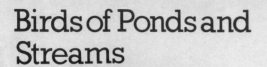

Many of the birds you see at ponds and streams are birds that can swim and perhaps dive for food. Most of them have webbed feet to propel themselves through the water. There may also be long-legged birds, like herons, that wade through the water. Some water birds nest on the water but most nest on the shore.

Several kinds of birds live among the reeds that often line the banks of ponds and streams. They hide there to escape danger and it is usually hard to spot them.

Other birds hunt from the air, chasing flying insects or plunging into the water to catch fish.

◄ **Kingfisher**
(16 cm) Darts over rivers and lakes, plunging to catch fishes.

▼ **Grey Heron**
(91 cm) Stands or wades in water, suddenly darting its beak into the water to capture prey.

▼ **Mute Swan**
(150 cm) Swims on lakes and rivers, lowering its long neck to feed underwater.

◄ **Reed Warbler**
(13 cm) Lives among reeds and low bushes beside the water.

◄ **Water Rail**
(28 cm) Slips through reeds, but seldom comes out into the open.

Male

Female

▲ **Mallard** (58 cm)
Common dabbling duck.

▲ **Pochard** (46 cm)
Diving duck.

▲ **Wigeon** (46 cm)
Dabbling duck.

▲ **Shoveler** (51 cm)
Dabbling duck.

▲ **Tufted Duck** (43 cm)
Diving duck.

▲ **Teal** (36 cm)
Dabbling duck.

▲ **Pintail** (63 cm)
Dabbling duck.

▲ **Greylag Goose** (84 cm)
Very common goose.

▲ **Canada Goose**
(97 cm)

◀ **Great Crested Grebe** (46 cm)
Dives for food and builds a floating nest.

▼ **Bittern** (76 cm)
Hides away in reeds near water; makes a booming call.

▲ **Moorhen** (33 cm) Swims bobbing its head, and sometimes diving.

◀ **Coot** (38 cm)
Nests at the water's edge.

71

Woodland Birds

Many birds make their homes in woodland. There is plenty of food to eat, and the birds can hide their nests among the leaves. Small birds, like tits and finches, clamber over the branches to find seeds, nuts and berries. Insect-eaters, such as warblers, flutter through the leaves. Woodpeckers pick insects from the bark of the trees and carve nest holes.

Owls swoop through the woods after dark and catch mice and other small animals. On the ground, other birds search through the undergrowth or scratch in the soil to find food.

▲ **Long-eared Owl** (36 cm) The 'ears' are tufts of feathers.

◀ **Crested Tit** (11 cm) Usually lives among pine and fir trees.

◀ **Coal Tit** (11 cm) Searches for insects and seeds.

▼ **Capercaillie** (86 cm) Huge grouse of conifer woods.

▲ **Goldcrest** (9 cm) Tiny bird mainly of conifer woods.

▼ **Crossbill** (16 cm) Opens fir cones to eat seeds.

▲ **Bullfinch** (15 cm) Likes to eat buds.

◀ **Sparrowhawk** (33 cm) Chases small birds through trees.

▲ **Blackcap** (14 cm) Hides away in bushes and undergrowth.

▲ **Treecreeper** (13 cm) Climbs trunks, seeking insects in the bark.

Woodpeckers

▲ **Black Wood-pecker** (46 cm)

▲ **Green Wood-pecker** (30 cm)

▲ **Great Spotted Woodpecker** (23 cm)

▲ **Lesser Spotted Wood-pecker** (15 cm)

▲ **Nightingale** (16 cm) Sings at night.

▶ **Woodpigeon** (41 cm) Seed eater, often seen in flocks.

▲ **Chiffchaff** (11 cm) Searches for insects high in the trees.

▲ **Great Tit** (14 cm) Seeks insects and seeds in all woods.

◀ **Tawny Owl** (38 cm) Common owl of woods.

▼ **Nuthatch** (14 cm) Makes nest hole in trees.

▲ **Pied Fly-catcher** (13 cm) Chases flying insects through woods.

▶ **Wood Warbler** (13 cm) Seeks insects among leaves.

▶ **Redstart** (14 cm) Insect eater of the woodland.

▼ **Jay** (36 cm) Buries acorns in the ground.

▲ **Woodcock** (36 cm) Digs in damp soil among trees.

Fields and Meadows

Many birds come to fields and meadows to feed from the plants and to peck for insects and worms. Not all of these birds make their permanent home on the ground. Some, like starlings, fly off to nearby trees or buildings to sleep and nest, and others *migrate* for the winter. However, many live on the ground all the time. They hide their nests among the grass and often roam in flocks over the fields in winter.

The hedgerows that border fields are the homes of several birds. Buntings and other small birds sing from the branches and hide their nests among them. Some birds are winter visitors that come to strip the bushes of their berries.

▲ **Little Owl** (23 cm) Hunts over fields, sometimes during the day.

▲ **Barn Owl** (36 cm) Seen in fields and farm-land at dusk.

◄ Owls have eyes that face forward to locate their prey.

► Most birds, like the meadow pipit, have eyes on the sides of their heads to spot enemies.

▼ **Lapwing** (30 cm) Roams over fields, often in large flocks.

▼ **Pheasant** (84 cm) Seen in fields mostly in winter. The female (foreground) is smaller and duller.

▼ **Quail** (18 cm) Hides away among grass.

▼ **Partridge** (30 cm) Wanders over fields, often in groups.

▲ **Cuckoo** (33 cm) Lays its eggs in the nests of other birds, which raise the young cuckoos.

▲ **Nightjar** (28 cm) Hunts flying insects by night, and hides away during the day.

▲ **Skylark** (18 cm) Lives on the ground in fields, hiding its nest among grass.

▲ **Yellow Wagtail** (16 cm) Usually seen in fields near water; nests on the ground.

▲ **Red-backed Shrike** (18 cm) Hunts over fields and hedges for insects and small birds.

▲ **Whitethroat** (14 cm) Darts through the air over fields and hedge-rows in summer.

▲ **Redwing** (20 cm) Comes to fields in winter, seeking berries to eat.

▲ **Fieldfare** (25 cm) Winter visitor to fields and hedges, searching for berries.

▲ **Goldfinch** (13 cm) Seen on fields in winter, often perching on thistles.

▲ **Corn Bunting** (18 cm) Lives in fields, hiding its nest in grass or low bushes.

▲ **Yellowhammer** (16 cm) Sings from bushes or hedges; seen on fields in winter.

▲ **Linnet** (13 cm) Nests in bushes and hedges; roams over fields in winter.

Mountains and Moorlands

Birds that make their homes in the mountains can fly well, for they must battle with the strong winds that howl around the high crags and over the valleys. Eagles and other *birds of prey* soar in the air, seeking victims on the ground below. Ravens and choughs tumble through the sky, on the look-out for almost anything that they can eat. Other birds live on the mountain slopes, seeking food among the rocks, on the sparse plants and in mountain streams.

Birds also survive on high moorlands. Many live among the grass, heather and other small plants.

▼ **Raven** (63 cm) Lives in mountains and other remote places, often feeding on dead animals.

▲ **Buzzard** (53 cm) Seen soaring over moors and mountain slopes, as well as in fields and woods.

▶ **Hooded Crow** (46 cm) Lives on moors and fields, where it eats almost anything it can find.

▼ **Dipper** (18 cm) Found at mountain streams and rivers, diving for food.

▶ **Meadow Pipit** (15 cm) Lives on moors and fields, hiding its nest on the ground.

▲ **Wheatear** (15 cm) Lives on moors and hillsides, nesting in holes.

▼ Great Grey Shrike (24 cm) Pursues insects, lizards and small birds.

▲ Golden Eagle (84 cm) Soars over mountain slopes, seeking rabbits and other prey.

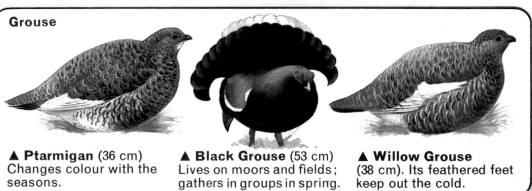

Grouse

▲ Ptarmigan (36 cm) Changes colour with the seasons.

▲ Black Grouse (53 cm) Lives on moors and fields; gathers in groups in spring.

▲ Willow Grouse (38 cm). Its feathered feet keep out the cold.

◀ Ring Ouzel (24 cm) Found on moors and mountain slopes, often among rocks.

▶ Golden Plover (28 cm) Found on moors in summer. It nests on the ground.

Seashore Birds

Few birds live on the seashore all the year round. Gulls can usually be seen at all times of the year, but most *seabirds* come ashore only in the spring and summer to raise their young. They nest on cliffs by the sea, or on pebble beaches where their eggs cannot be easily seen. These seabirds fish in the sea, either diving from the air, as terns do, or from the surface, like cormorants. Some even snatch food from the water while still in the air.

In the winter, these seabirds fly out to sea. Birds such as ducks and sandpipers come to the coast from inland. They dive for shellfish offshore, or look for food on the beach.

Gulls and Terns

Common Gull (41 cm)

Herring Gull (56 cm)

Lesser Black-backed Gull (53 cm)

Common Tern (34 cm)

Little Tern (24 cm)

▼ **Curlew** (56 cm) Seen on mudflats in winter.

◄ **Avocet** (43 cm) Wades in shallows, feeding in water.

▼ **Common Sandpiper** (20 cm) Comes to wade on the shore in winter.

▼ **Dunlin** (18 cm) At the coast in winter in large flocks.

▼ **Sanderling** (20 cm) Seen racing over sandy beaches in winter.

◄ **Knot** (25 cm) Found in flocks on mudflats in winter.

▲ **Ringed Plover** (19 cm) Found on beaches all the year.

▼ **Fulmar** (46 cm)
Nests on cliffs and
follows ships at
sea.

► **Gannet** (91 cm)
Nests on cliffs
and dives for fish
offshore.

◄ **Shelduck**
(61 cm) Goose-
like duck found at
muddy and sandy
beaches. Often
nests in a hole
near the shore, and
gathers in huge
flocks to moult.

► **Guillemot**
(41 cm) Nests on
cliffs, laying pear-
shaped egg on a
bare ledge of
rock.

► **Cormorant**
(91 cm) Flies low
over sea before
settling and then
diving for fish.

► **Shag** (76 cm)
Like a small
cormorant, but
does not have
white markings
on its head.

▲ **Razorbill**
(41 cm) Comes to
cliffs to nest in
huge colonies.

◄ **Puffin** (30 cm)
Nests in burrow
on a cliff.

▲ **Oystercatcher**
(43 cm) Feeds on
shellfish on the
shore.

79

Birds of Towns and Gardens

Garden Birds

▲ **Dunnock** (15 cm) Often seen in hedges and flower beds.

▲ **Greenfinch** (15 cm) Often found in garden trees and bushes.

▲ **Blue Tit** (11 cm) Common in woods and gardens.

▲ **Long-tailed Tit** (14 cm) Makes globe-shaped nest.

▲ **Wren** (10 cm) Scurries over ground and walls.

▲ **Robin** (14 cm) Hops over ground, pecking for food.

A few birds, such as the house sparrow and the feral pigeon, can make their homes in the centre of a city. They get food from people, and can nest under the eaves of roofs, in holes in walls or on the ledges of buildings. Starlings often come to a city centre to sleep on ledges, but during the day they fly out to feed in parks and gardens, or in the surrounding countryside.

Parks and gardens have many more birds. Here, the birds can find their own food. There are also trees and bushes in which to nest without being disturbed.

For many birds, it is better to live in towns than in the country. They escape many of the enemies that hunt them in the wild, and they may get food and shelter from people, especially in winter.

Thrushes

▲ **Mistle Thrush** (28 cm) Often seen in parks and gardens.

▲ **Song Thrush** (23 cm) Very common bird of parks and gardens.

▲ **Redwing** (20 cm) Garden bird of northern Europe.

▲ **Blackbird** (25 cm) Female is brown. Very common in gardens.

▲ **Kestrel** (33 cm) Hovers in the air, then dives after small animals.

▲ **Swift** (16 cm)

▶ **Black-headed Gull** (38 cm) Head goes white in winter.

▼ **House Sparrow** (15 cm) Very common town bird.

▶ **Feral Pigeon** (33 cm) Found throughout towns. Plumage may vary.

▶ **Starling** (21 cm) Loses white spots in spring and summer.

▶ **Swallow** (19 cm) Flies low, seeking flying insects.

▶ **House Martin** (13 cm) Makes a mud nest under eaves.

▲ **Collared Dove** (30 cm) Recent arrival in Europe.

▲ **Pied Wagtail** (18 cm) Comes to buildings to nest and to sleep.

Carrion Crow (46 cm)

Magpie (46 cm)

Rook (46 cm)

Finding Clues

Finding things which birds have left behind will give you a clue to which ones have been in an area. The most common clues are feathers and pellets (see below). At first, you may have difficulty in identifying them. But after some practice they will become easier to recognize.

Sometimes you will find the chewed remains of nuts and cones. They are the food of other animals, as well as birds, so be careful how you identify what has eaten them. Birds usually leave jagged holes while other animals chew neat ones.

You will probably want to make a collection of the things that you have found. Individual feathers can be stuck in a notebook and labelled (see opposite). Wings cut from dead birds can also be collected. If there is any flesh left on the wing you will need to rub it with salt or borax to preserve it. You can then dry the wing and store it (see opposite). Remember to wash your hands after handling pellets, feathers and wings.

You must never collect bird's eggs and never go near a nest when it contains eggs or young. In the autumn, when the *breeding season* is over, you can study the nest.

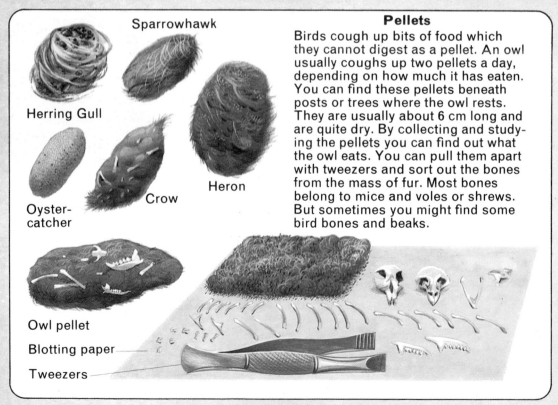

Sparrowhawk

Herring Gull

Oyster-catcher

Crow

Heron

Owl pellet

Blotting paper

Tweezers

Pellets

Birds cough up bits of food which they cannot digest as a pellet. An owl usually coughs up two pellets a day, depending on how much it has eaten. You can find these pellets beneath posts or trees where the owl rests. They are usually about 6 cm long and are quite dry. By collecting and studying the pellets you can find out what the owl eats. You can pull them apart with tweezers and sort out the bones from the mass of fur. Most bones belong to mice and voles or shrews. But sometimes you might find some bird bones and beaks.

▲ **Feathers** that you find can be collected and put in a notebook, like the mallard feather shown above. You can write notes beside each feather.

▲ **Wings** cut from dead birds can be pinned on a piece of cardboard and left for a few days to dry. They can then be stored in a paper bag with a label and mothballs.

Wood Pigeon

Curlew

Herring Gull

Pheasant

Jay

Swan

Below, left to right: hover-fly, puss moth caterpillar, longhorn beetle, southern aeshna dragonfly.

INSECTS

Insects are the commonest creatures on Earth. There are probably about one million different kinds. Few insects actually live in the sea, but you can find them just about everywhere else. Some insects damage our crops, but there are many others that do good, or whose beauty brightens up our countryside.

The next few pages will help you identify many of the commoner insects that you can find in your home or garden, or on a walk. Some people make collections of insects, but you will learn much more about the way these fascinating creatures behave if you let them stay in their natural surroundings and study them there.

What to Look For

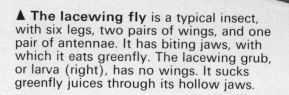

▲ **The lacewing fly** is a typical insect, with six legs, two pairs of wings, and one pair of antennae. It has biting jaws, with which it eats greenfly. The lacewing grub, or larva (right), has no wings. It sucks greenfly juices through its hollow jaws.

Despite the enormous variety of insect shapes and sizes, it is easy to recognise an adult insect: its body is always divided into three parts. These are the head, the thorax, and the abdomen. On the head is a pair of antennae, or feelers, and usually two large compound eyes made up of many tiny lenses. Different insects have different kinds of mouths to suit their particular diets. Some have biting jaws to chew solid food, others suck up liquids.

On the thorax are three pairs of legs, and most adult insects also have wings. The form of the wings will help you to identify insects. Flies have only two wings, but most other insects have four. Be careful when counting wings: beetles, bugs, and some other insects have hard front wings that cover most of the body and hide the delicate hind wings. Do not be fooled into thinking these insects are wingless.

Many young insects look very different from the adults and change as they grow up. The change from young to adult form is called metamorphosis. It often takes place during a resting stage known as the pupa or chrysalis.

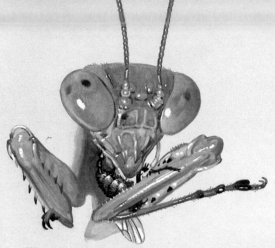

▲ **The praying mantis** spots its prey with its great eyes, catches it with spiky front legs, and chews it with powerful jaws.

► **Scorpion fly**
The harmless scorpion fly has two pairs of narrow wings.

◄ **Mayfly**
This mayfly has only one pair of wings. Most species have two pairs.

► **Flea**
The flea is quite wingless. Wings would be a hindrance to this fur-dwelling parasite.

◄ **Earwig**
Some earwigs have wings, but usually keep them folded away out of sight.

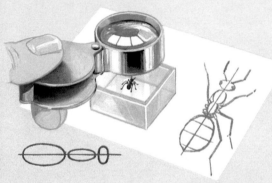

▲ **A hand lens** magnifying ten times is useful for studying insects. You can draw insects by using three ovals.

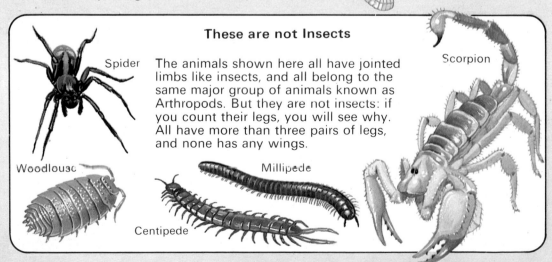

These are not Insects

Spider

The animals shown here all have jointed limbs like insects, and all belong to the same major group of animals known as Arthropods. But they are not insects: if you count their legs, you will see why. All have more than three pairs of legs, and none has any wings.

Scorpion

Woodlouse

Millipede

Centipede

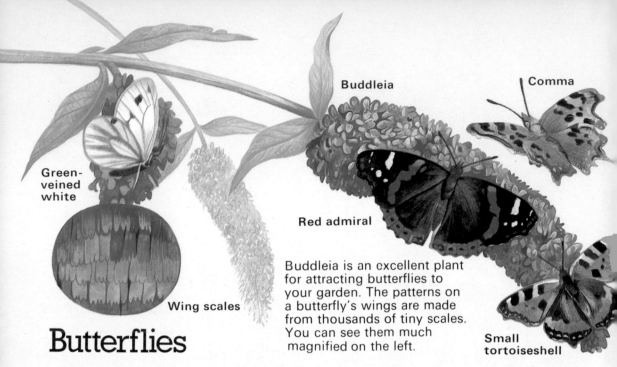

Buddleia

Comma

Green-
veined
white

Red admiral

Wing scales

Small
tortoiseshell

Buddleia is an excellent plant for attracting butterflies to your garden. The patterns on a butterfly's wings are made from thousands of tiny scales. You can see them much magnified on the left.

Butterflies

Butterflies are among the most beautiful insects, and you can attract many species to your garden by planting nectar-rich flowers for them to feed on. You can watch them plunging their long tongues into the flowers to suck up the nectar. When they are not feeding, their tongues are coiled up.

Butterflies belong to the same group of insects as moths. The wings of both groups are covered with tiny scales that come off if you touch them. Butterflies fly by day, and their antennae have clubbed tips. Most moths fly at night, and their antennae are thread-like or feathery, but there are some day-flying moths and a few have clubbed antennae.

Female butterflies lay their eggs on leaves. The eggs hatch into tiny caterpillars which feed on the leaves and grow steadily. They change their skins, or moult, several times and then turn into chrysalises, or pupae. Inside the chrysalis the caterpillar changes form and eventually emerges as an adult butterfly.

▼ **Painted lady** feeding on ice-plant flowers.

▼ **Peacock** butterfly's life cycle.

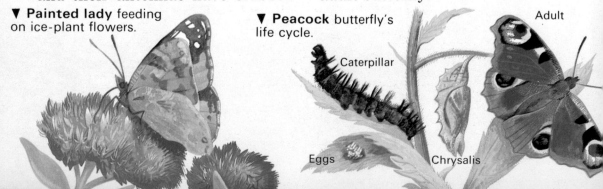

Adult

Caterpillar

Eggs

Chrysalis

WOODLAND BUTTERFLIES

Speckled wood

Ringlet

White admiral

Purple hairstreak

Orange tip

Silver washed fritillary

Gatekeeper

Brimstone

BUTTERFLIES OF THE FIELDS

Wall brown

Meadow brown

Small heath

Marbled white

Swallowtail

Grizzled skipper

Small copper

Clouded yellow

Chalkhill blue

Common blue

Heath fritillary

Dark green fritillary

Moths

▲ **Hummingbird hawk moth**
flies by day. It sucks
nectar from deep-throated
flowers.

Moths are closely related to butterflies, but most of them fly by night.
Many have very long tongues to
reach the nectar in deep-throated
flowers like the honeysuckle.
Others have no tongue at all and
do not feed in the adult stage.
They build up all the food reserves
they need while they are caterpillars.

Moths rest by day, often on tree
trunks or leaves. They are usually
so well camouflaged that birds
cannot find them. Many moth
caterpillars are also beautifully
camouflaged, some of them looking
remarkably like twigs.

Moth caterpillars grow up just
like butterfly caterpillars, but when
they are fully grown they usually
spin silken cocoons around themselves or burrow in the ground to
pupate.

▲ **Green carpet moth** rests on tree
trunks by day and is very hard to see.

▼ **Moth-trap** Moths are attracted into
the trap by the bright light.

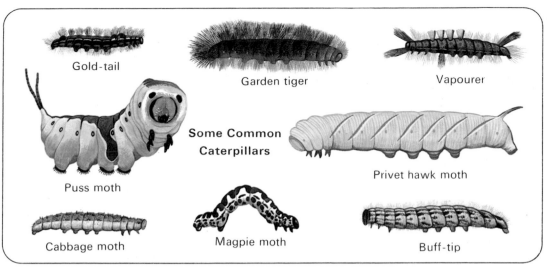

Gold-tail

Garden tiger

Vapourer

Some Common Caterpillars

Puss moth

Privet hawk moth

Cabbage moth

Magpie moth

Buff-tip

Some Moths that can be found in your Garden

Garden carpet

Common emerald

Swallowtailed

Blood-vein

Tawny speckled pug

Garden tiger

6-spot burnet

Cinnabar

Common magpie

Peppered moth

Eyed hawk moth

Silver Y

Drinker

Brimstone moth

Scalloped oak

Large yellow underwing

Bugs and Beetles

Beetles and bugs are often confused because they live in similar places and both have fairly hard front wings that cover much of their bodies. In fact, they are very different. Beetles have biting jaws, and their hard front wings meet in a straight line down the centre of the body. Young beetles are called larvae and they have no wings. They pass through a pupa stage before becoming adult. Beetles eat a very wide variety of foods, including other small animals, living and dead plants, and dung.

Bugs have sucking mouths like minute drinking straws or hypodermic needles. They stick their mouths into other animals or plants and suck up the juices. Many bugs, including the familiar greenfly and blackfly, carry plant diseases. Greenfly and blackfly have flimsy wings, but most bugs have hard front wings. Unlike those of beetles, they overlap on the insect's back. Bugs have no pupa stage.

▲ **Ladybird** folding its hind wings under its tough front wings after flight.

▶ **Head of a beetle** with strong biting jaws.

◀ **Rose chafer**

◀ **Ladybird** eating greenfly

▼ **Burying beetles** bury dead animals and lay eggs on them

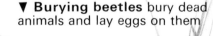

▲ **Leaf beetles**

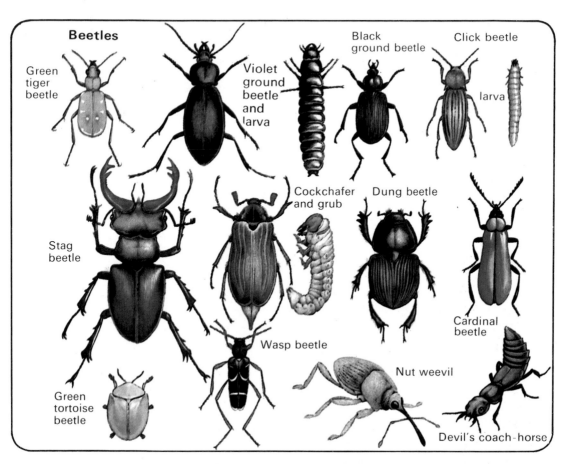

Beetles

Green tiger beetle

Violet ground beetle and larva

Black ground beetle

Click beetle

larva

Stag beetle

Cockchafer and grub

Dung beetle

Cardinal beetle

Green tortoise beetle

Wasp beetle

Nut weevil

Devil's coach-horse

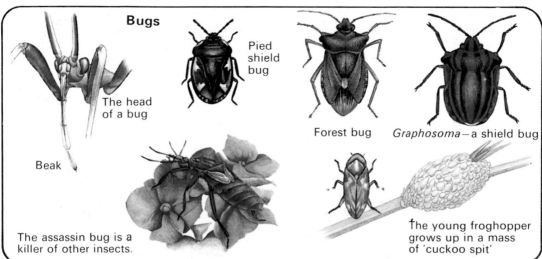

Bugs

The head of a bug

Beak

Pied shield bug

Forest bug

Graphosoma — a shield bug

The assassin bug is a killer of other insects.

The young froghopper grows up in a mass of 'cuckoo spit'

Flies

The true flies are a very large group of insects with a great range of sizes. Some crane-flies, or daddy-long-legs, have bodies over 3 cm long and wingspans of more than 5 cm. At the other end of the scale there are midges smaller than a pin head. Flies never have more than one pair of wings. The hind wings are simply a pair of tiny,

◄ **Crane-flies,** also called daddy-long-legs, are common in fields and gardens in autumn. The balancing organs can be seen near the wing bases. Adult crane-flies rarely feed, but their larvae, known as leatherjackets, eat lots of plant roots in the soil.

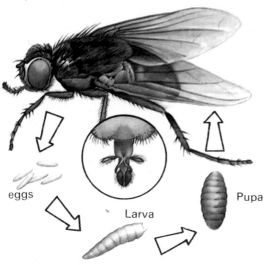

eggs

Larva

Pupa

▲ **Houseflies** lay their eggs in decaying matter. The life cycle can be complete in a week in warm weather. The sponge-like mouth is drawn in the circle.

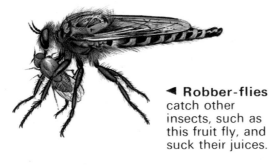

◄ **Robber-flies** catch other insects, such as this fruit fly, and suck their juices.

pin-like balancing organs called halteres. You will see these easily if you look at a large crane-fly.

All flies eat liquid foods, but they feed in several different ways. Some, such as the hover-fly, suck nectar from flowers. Others have piercing beaks through which they suck blood from other animals. They can sometimes transmit diseases to their victims as they feed on them. Houseflies and bluebottles have 'sponge-like' mouths to sop up their food. They can eat solid materials, such as cake and meat, by pouring saliva over them and mopping up the solution.

The grubs that hatch from flies' eggs are called larvae. They are very different from the adults. They are all legless and live in an amazing variety of places. Some live in the soil and eat plant roots, others live in dung or inside plants and animals, and many live in water.

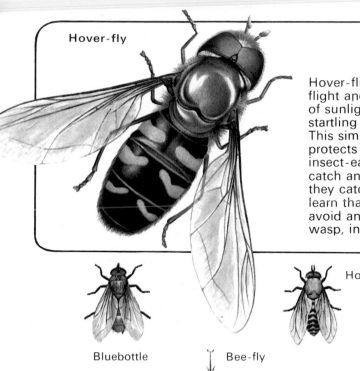

Hover-fly

Mimicry

Hover-flies are famed for their darting flight and their ability to hover in shafts of sunlight. Many of them also bear a startling resemblance to bees and wasps. This similarity is called mimicry, and it protects the hover-flies from many insect-eating birds. Young birds try to catch and eat almost anything, but when they catch bees and wasps they soon learn that they get stung. After that, they avoid anything that looks like a bee or a wasp, including the harmless hover-flies.

Bluebottle

Horse-fly

Greenbottle

Bee-fly

Soldier-fly

Hover-fly

Cluster-fly

Sheep ked

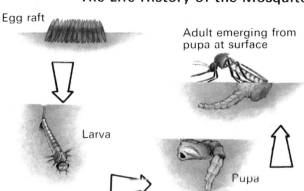

The Life History of the Mosquito

Egg raft

Adult emerging from pupa at surface

Larva

Pupa

Female mosquitos lay their eggs on the water surface and the larvae grow up in the water.

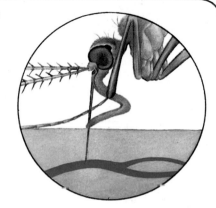

Only the female mosquito sucks blood. Her sharp beak easily penetrates our skin.

Insects that Live Together

Most insects live alone and have no real homes, but ants and termites are different. They live in colonies, sometimes with millions of other individuals in one nest.

Some ants build their nests underground. Others build a mound of soil and leaves on the surface. Inside, there are many passages and chambers. Some chambers are larders, some are nurseries, and some may be cemeteries. The colony is ruled by a queen, who lays all the eggs. She has wings when she is young, but she breaks them off before starting a nest. Most of the ants are wingless females called workers. They build and repair the nest and feed the queen and the young. Some species also have other extra large workers, called soldiers, to defend the nest. Male ants are winged and appear only in summer, when clouds of them emerge for mating flights with the new queens.

Many bees and wasps live in colonies. They are also ruled by queens, but both the queen and the workers are always winged. Bees feed their young on pollen and nectar, while wasps rear their young on animal food.

Termite colonies have kings as well as queens. The work is done by young termites of both sexes, many of which never grow up completely. The soldiers are also of both sexes.

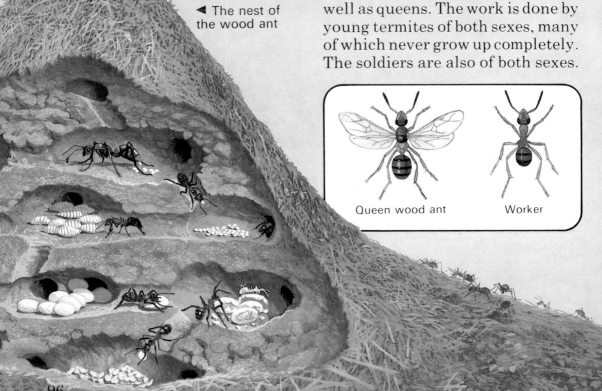

◄ The nest of the wood ant

Queen wood ant   Worker

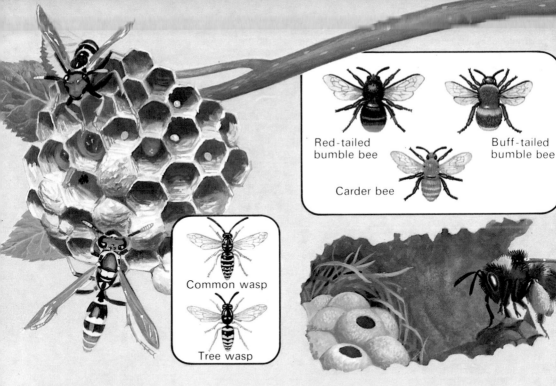

Red-tailed bumble bee

Buff-tailed bumble bee

Carder bee

Common wasp

Tree wasp

▲ **Social wasps,** such as this paper wasp, make their nests with chewed-up wood. An egg is laid in each cell.

▼ **Honeybees** build thousands of wax cells. They store honey and pollen in some and rear young in others.

▲ **Bumble bees** nest on or under the ground, often in an old mouse hole. Like wasps, their colonies last for just one season.

▼ **Termites** Some species live in dead wood and gradually eat it away. Others live in huge mounds of soil.

Queen

Worker

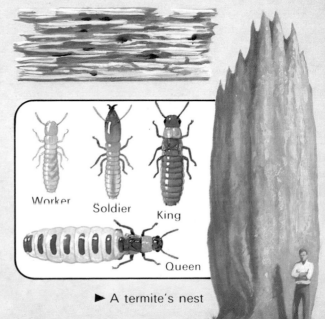

Worker

Soldier

King

Queen

► A termite's nest

Insects of the Waterside

Many insects live in and around ponds and streams. Some of them, such as water beetles and water scorpions, spend all their lives in the water. Others, such as dragonflies, mayflies, caddis flies and some midges, spend their early lives in the water but leave before turning into adults.

Dragonfly and mayfly young are called nymphs. They look similar to the adults but have under-developed wings. Unlike midge and caddis fly larvae, they do not pupate before becoming adult but undergo a gradual change. The final change takes place when the nymph climbs out of the water on to a reed. Its skin splits open and the adult insect struggles out.

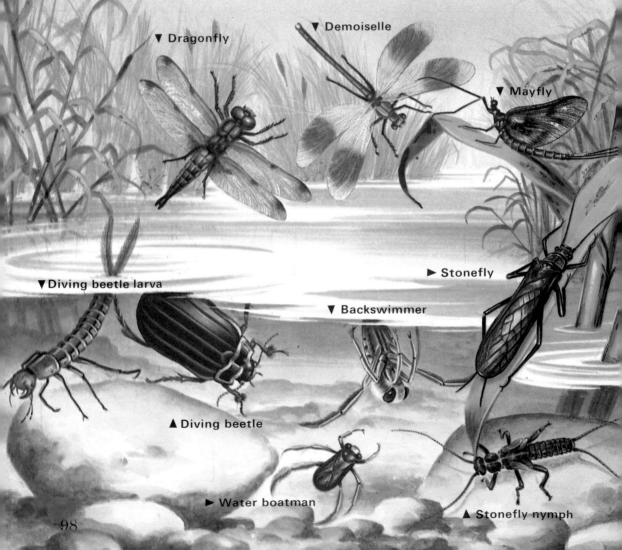

▼ Dragonfly

▼ Demoiselle

▼ Mayfly

▼ Diving beetle larva

► Stonefly

▼ Backswimmer

▲ Diving beetle

► Water boatman

▲ Stonefly nymph

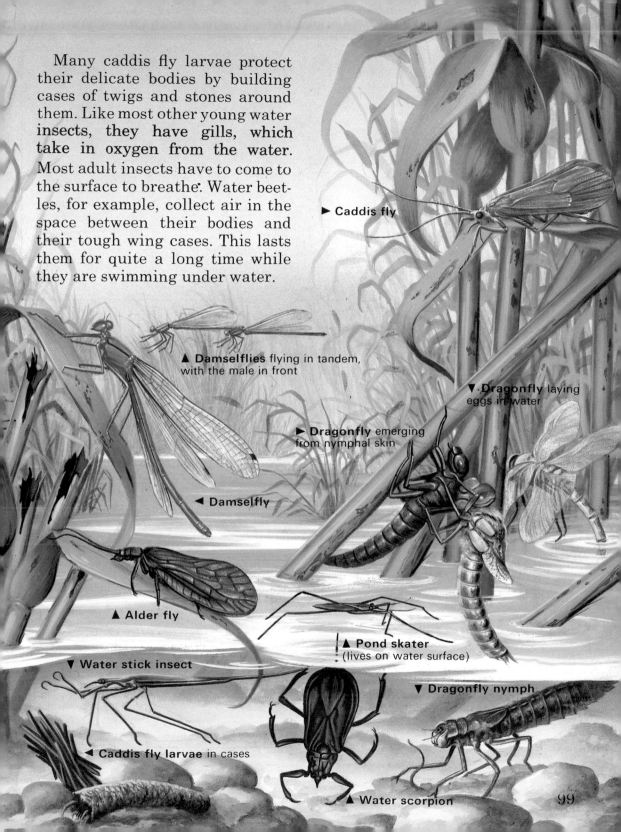

Many caddis fly larvae protect their delicate bodies by building cases of twigs and stones around them. Like most other young water insects, they have gills, which take in oxygen from the water. Most adult insects have to come to the surface to breathe. Water beetles, for example, collect air in the space between their bodies and their tough wing cases. This lasts them for quite a long time while they are swimming under water.

► **Caddis fly**

▲ **Damselflies** flying in tandem, with the male in front

▼ **Dragonfly** laying eggs in water

► **Dragonfly** emerging from nymphal skin

◄ **Damselfly**

▲ **Alder fly**

▲ **Pond skater** (lives on water surface)

▼ **Water stick insect**

▼ **Dragonfly nymph**

◄ **Caddis fly larvae** in cases

▲ **Water scorpion**

99

Drummers

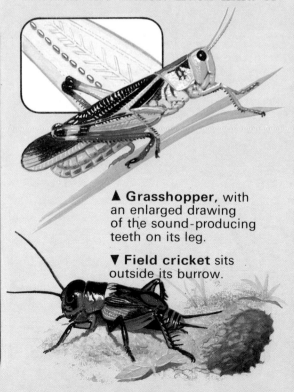

muscle

membrane

Cicadas are sap-sucking insects. The males are very noisy. A membrane on each side of the body vibrates at high speed like a miniature drum-skin. This produces a shrill, whistle-like sound which attracts the females.

The Ventriloquist

The Italian cricket lives in southern Europe. The male normally lifts his wings right up to produce his sweet, bubbling song, but he lowers them a little if he is disturbed. He continues singing in this position, but the sound is much softer. This makes it appear to be coming from further away than it actually is. With luck his enemies are fooled and he is safe.

Italian cricket

Sounds and Light

Many animals make use of sounds during their courtship. Among the insects, the best known 'singers' are the grasshoppers and crickets. Grasshoppers 'sing', or stridulate, to use the proper word, by rubbing their back legs against their wings. On the inner edge of the leg is a row of tiny teeth. These are scraped over a hard vein on the wing as the leg moves up and down. This sets the wing vibrating and produces the familiar buzz, or chirp. Only males chirp, and even then, usually only in sunshine. The females, attracted by the sounds, move towards the males. Each kind of

▲ **Grasshopper,** with an enlarged drawing of the sound-producing teeth on its leg.

▼ **Field cricket** sits outside its burrow.

grasshopper has its own song, and the females take no notice of the songs of other species.

Crickets chirp by rubbing one wing base over the other. Many have no proper wings, just little flaps which they rub together. The field cricket chirps in bright sunshine, but most crickets chirp in the evening. In some species the female, as well as the male, chirps.

Crickets have much longer antennae than grasshoppers, and the females have long, sword-like egg-laying tubes. Crickets and grasshoppers grow up without a pupa stage. Their bodies grow and their wings develop each time they moult until they finally emerge as adults.

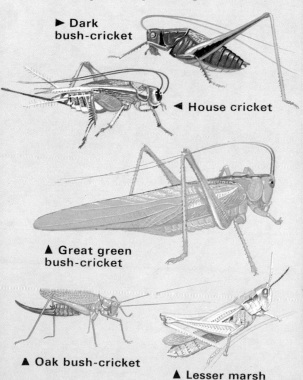

▶ **Dark bush-cricket**

◀ **House cricket**

▲ **Great green bush-cricket**

▲ **Oak bush-cricket**

▲ **Lesser marsh grasshopper**

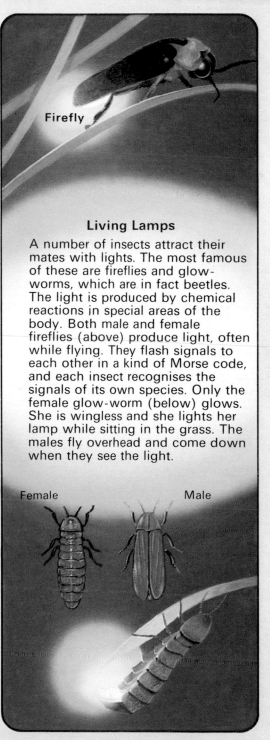

Firefly

Living Lamps

A number of insects attract their mates with lights. The most famous of these are fireflies and glow-worms, which are in fact beetles. The light is produced by chemical reactions in special areas of the body. Both male and female fireflies (above) produce light, often while flying. They flash signals to each other in a kind of Morse code, and each insect recognises the signals of its own species. Only the female glow-worm (below) glows. She is wingless and she lights her lamp while sitting in the grass. The males fly overhead and come down when they see the light.

Female   Male

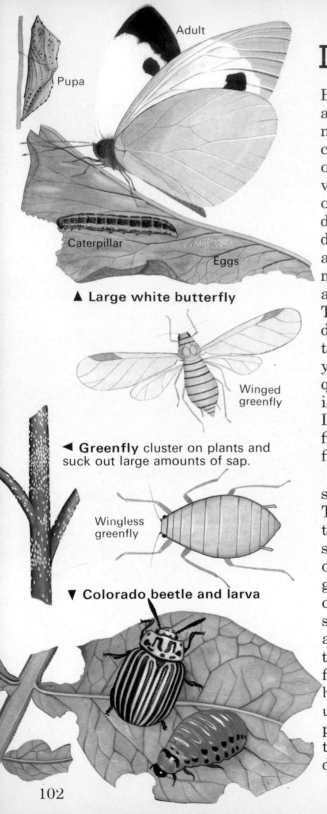

▲ Large white butterfly

Pupa

Adult

Caterpillar

Eggs

Winged greenfly

◄ Greenfly cluster on plants and suck out large amounts of sap.

Wingless greenfly

▼ Colorado beetle and larva

Insect Pests

Because insects are so numerous and so varied in their diets, it is not surprising that many of them come into conflict with man. Many of them eat our food; some eat the very wood with which we build our houses; others attack us or our domestic animals, often spreading diseases as they feed. These insects are all pests, and they destroy millions of pounds worth of food and other materials every year. Thousands of people also die from diseases carried by insects. Among these diseases are malaria and yellow fever, both carried by mosquitos, and sleeping sickness which is carried by tsetse-flies in Africa. Lice can carry typhus fever, while fleas can transmit plague. Rabbit fleas carry myxomatosis.

A great deal of time and effort is spent in controlling insect pests. The main method of controlling them is with poisons, called insecticides. These can be sprayed on to crops, or mixed with stored grain to kill the pests. Timber, clothes and carpets can also be sprayed with insecticides to kill any pests that land on them and try to eat them. Another method of fighting insect pests is known as biological control. This involves using the natural enemies of the pests—usually other insects—to kill them and so keep their numbers down.

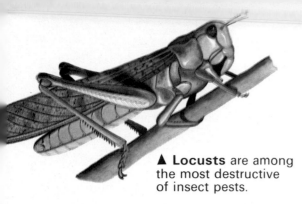

▲ **Locusts** are among the most destructive of insect pests.

▼ **Grain weevils** destroy vast quantities of stored grain.

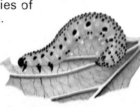

▲ **Gooseberry sawfly larva** strips gooseberry leaves.

▼ **Cockroaches** damage a wide variety of stored foods.

Wood Eaters

▲ **Elm bark beetle** The larvae tunnel under bark (above). The adults carry Dutch elm disease.

◀ **House longhorn beetle** The larvae destroy timber (above).

▲ **Deathwatch beetle** The larva is a serious pest of building timbers.

Insects that Feed on Man

▼ **Human flea** A blood sucker only in the adult stage.

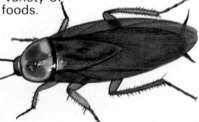

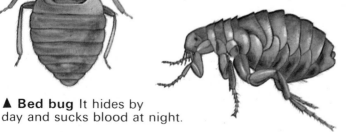

▲ **Bed bug** It hides by day and sucks blood at night.

▲ **Human louse** holds on with its big claws.

Below, starting top left: red squirrel, red deer, hedgehogs, pine marten, otter, mole, badgers, rabbit, dormouse.

MAMMALS

There are not many mammals, compared with the vast numbers of birds, insects or flowers. Also, many mammals are shy and difficult to see or watch. This is because they are afraid of their enemies, especially man. For a long time, people have hunted and killed them, either for food, or because they ate their crops or killed their domestic animals.

You do need to be very patient and quiet to watch mammals. This chapter tells you many fascinating facts about some of them, but there is still much that we do not know about how they live and behave. If you watch mammals carefully and note down what you see, you may help to add to our knowledge of these fascinating creatures.

Guard hairs

Underfur

▲ When otters come out of the water, their coats dry quickly, because water runs off their long guard hairs.

Stoat in summer

Stoat in winter

What are Mammals?

Mammals have several things in common. They are the only animals with *hair*. A soft, dense underfur keeps the animal warm, and the outer fur is made up of long, coarse *guard hairs*. Rain runs off these so the animal keeps dry. Dogs and cats make these hairs stand on end to look bigger and more impressive to an enemy.

Whiskers are special hairs used for feeling. With the hedgehog, hairs have now become protective spines. When the hedgehog rolls up, the spines protect it.

Hairs can be different colours. Those underneath the body are often lighter than those on the back. This contrast in colour helps to hide (*camouflage*) the animal against its background. Patterns of colours, too, break up the animal's shape. This makes it difficult to see, like spotted fallow deer in a wood where dappled sunlight comes through the trees. Some sea mammals, such as seals and whales, have no hair or only a few bristles. Instead, they keep themselves warm with a thick layer of fat (*blubber*) under the skin.

◄ Mammals moult (shed their hair) twice a year. The winter coat is long and thick to keep the animal warm. It is often a different colour to the summer coat. Roe deer have a grey-brown winter coat and a foxy-red summer coat. Some animals, like the stoat, turn white in the winter but only when the weather gets very cold. Young animals are often a different colour to the adult. They moult to grow their adult coats.

All mammals feed their young on *milk*. Before they are born, the babies grow inside the mother. Some mammal babies are born without fur and are deaf and blind. They are usually born in nests or burrows. They stay in these until they have grown hair and their eyes and ears have opened. Some mammals, like rabbits and mice, breed quickly and have several families a year, and many young are born at the same time.

Others carry their young inside them for a longer time, and have only a small family. These babies are born with hair, can see, hear and walk, and follow their mother very soon after birth. These young mammals often have camouflaging coats to hide them from enemies.

▶ Young deer can stand up and run soon after birth. At first they lie still in bushes. Their spotted coats make them hard to see. The mother comes to feed them, until they are strong enough to follow her.

107

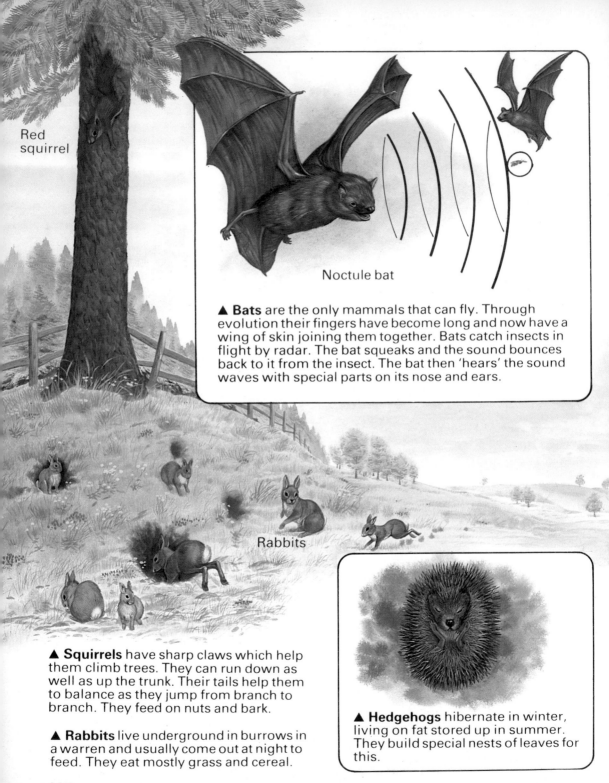

Red squirrel

Noctule bat

▲ **Bats** are the only mammals that can fly. Through evolution their fingers have become long and now have a wing of skin joining them together. Bats catch insects in flight by radar. The bat squeaks and the sound bounces back to it from the insect. The bat then 'hears' the sound waves with special parts on its nose and ears.

Rabbits

▲ **Squirrels** have sharp claws which help them climb trees. They can run down as well as up the trunk. Their tails help them to balance as they jump from branch to branch. They feed on nuts and bark.

▲ **Rabbits** live underground in burrows in a warren and usually come out at night to feed. They eat mostly grass and cereal.

▲ **Hedgehogs** hibernate in winter, living on fat stored up in summer. They build special nests of leaves for this.

Ways of Living

Animals live in many different ways. The study of how they live in their surroundings is called *ecology*. Some go about in groups, and so they can help each other. Deer in herds can graze safely, knowing that some of them are keeping a watch for enemies. Wolves live in packs, helping each other to hunt and bring up their young. Groups have a leader, and all the animals know their own place in it.

▼ **Wolf** (1.5 m). Looks like a large grey Alsatian dog.

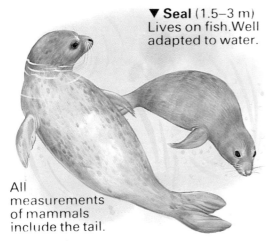

▼ **Seal** (1.5–3 m) Lives on fish. Well adapted to water.

All measurements of mammals include the tail.

Seals are mammals that live in the sea, but are sometimes seen in rivers. They are sleek and stream-lined to swim easily through the water. All animals form part of *food webs* which show how they depend on other living things. Here is the seal's food web: small sea plants are eaten by small sea animals, which are then eaten by fish. The fish are eaten by the seals, which are eaten by Eskimoes.

A number of animals have learned to live near people, making use of their food and buildings. Many years ago, brown rats came to Europe from Asia in ships. Rats carry diseases and are a danger to people's health. They eat food stored for people and animals and spoil much more with their droppings. With their sharp front teeth, rats gnaw and damage doors, floors and metal pipes.

▼ **Rat** (40 cm) Lives in fields in summer.

What to Look For

Many animals are shy and only come out at night. Often all that we see are the signs that they leave behind them. *Tracks* from their feet are obvious clues, but there are many other signs as well.

Some animals have *homes* which are easily seen, like the squirrel's drey. A drey with fresh leaves woven into it is being used. Deer leave the grass flat where they have been lying. Bedding of grass and leaves outside a badger's sett shows that the sett is being lived in. Scratches on trees show an animal has sharpened its claws. Scrapes in soil show where a rabbit has been.

Animals also leave *food remains*, pine cones gnawed by squirrels and nuts nibbled by mice. Otters leave half-eaten fish on river banks. Short grass or corn at the edge of fields has been grazed by deer or rabbits.

Different kinds of animals leave *droppings* of different shapes. Fresh droppings are moist, with flies round them in warm weather. Some animals scatter droppings anywhere, but a fox will leave them on a stone or log, while badgers bury theirs in special places.

Sounds and *smells* also tell us if animals are about. Roe deer bark if frightened. Foxes bark like a dog and vixens scream. Hedgehogs snuffle in hedges at dusk. Foxes also leave a scent where they have passed.

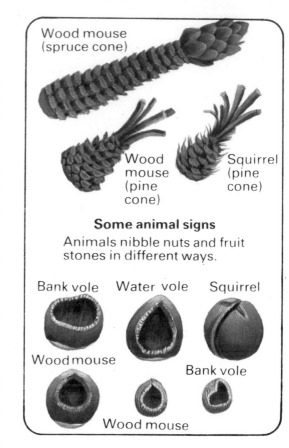

Wood mouse (spruce cone)

Wood mouse (pine cone)

Squirrel (pine cone)

Some animal signs

Animals nibble nuts and fruit stones in different ways.

Bank vole   Water vole   Squirrel

Wood mouse

Bank vole

Wood mouse

▼ This fox's earth is probably in use, because there are no cobwebs round it.

SKULLS

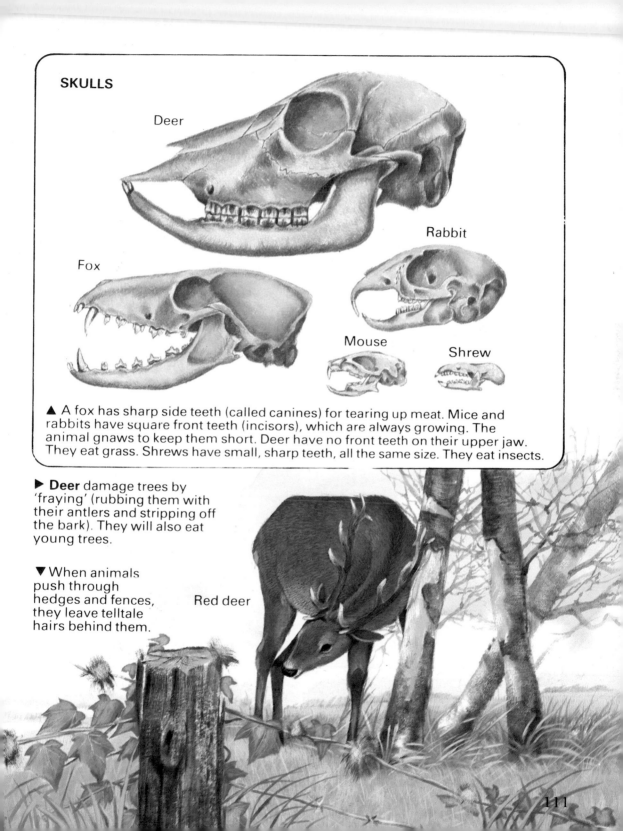

Deer

Rabbit

Fox

Mouse

Shrew

▲ A fox has sharp side teeth (called canines) for tearing up meat. Mice and rabbits have square front teeth (incisors), which are always growing. The animal gnaws to keep them short. Deer have no front teeth on their upper jaw. They eat grass. Shrews have small, sharp teeth, all the same size. They eat insects.

▶ **Deer** damage trees by 'fraying' (rubbing them with their antlers and stripping off the bark). They will also eat young trees.

▼ When animals push through hedges and fences, they leave telltale hairs behind them.

Red deer

Tracks and Signs

The most obvious signs an animal leaves behind are its tracks – (marks of hooves or paws). Complete footprints can only be seen in soft muddy ground, sand or snow. On hard ground only part of the print is left. Tracks of larger animals are easier to recognize than the smaller prints of mice, shrews and voles.

The tracks of the same kind of animal may differ from each other. A heavy red deer stag (male) leaves more distinct prints than the lighter hind (female). Tracks of young animals are smaller than adult prints. Footprints of old

▼ **Deer tracks** are called slots. Front footprints are smaller than the hind feet. Footprints of sheep are broader.

Walking

▼ **Badger tracks** show five toe marks and a long bar-shaped main pad.

▼ **Fox tracks** have four round toes, same size and shape as main pad.

▼ **Dog tracks:** four toes and a main pad which is triangular in shape.

112

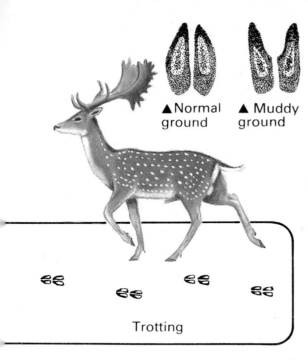

▲Normal ground ▲ Muddy ground

Trotting

animals may show marks of long, overgrown claws.

Tracks also tell us what the animals were doing. A fox will keep to the cover of bushes – unlike a dog. Three footprints show an animal was hurt in one leg. You can also see how fast an animal was moving: walking, trotting or galloping. Prints when walking are close together, but the faster the animal goes, the further apart they become. Fresh tracks are easy to see; old ones fill up with dust.

If you go out at dawn or dusk, and keep very quiet, you may see some mammals. You can also attract some like hedgehogs with food.

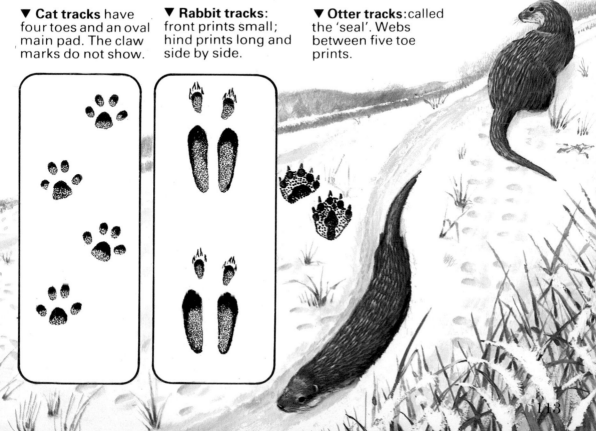

▼ **Cat tracks** have four toes and an oval main pad. The claw marks do not show.

▼ **Rabbit tracks:** front prints small; hind prints long and side by side.

▼ **Otter tracks**: called the 'seal'. Webs between five toe prints.

113

▲ **Badgers** (75 cm) Dig out large burrows called setts.

▲ **Squirrels** (46 cm) Build dreys in trees, often in a fork.

Woodlands

The kind of place where an animal lives is called its *habitat*. Woodlands provide a habitat for many different kinds of animals. Some hide in the woods during the day and venture out into fields and clearings at night to feed. Such animals are called *nocturnal*. Their enemies cannot see them so easily at night. Other animals may usually feed at dawn or dusk. Where they are not disturbed, they can also be seen during the day.

Different animals live at different *levels* in a wood. The wood mouse burrows underground, and so does the badger. Both come out at night to feed. Deer hide in woods during the day and feed at dawn and dusk.

Foxes rest in woods during the day and hunt in the surrounding fields at night.

Other animals, such as squirrels and pine martens, live in trees, feeding there as well as on the ground. Bats use hollow trees to roost, flying out to catch insects in the evenings.

Animals also have *territories* in which they live and feed. They mark the edges of their territory so that other animals of the same kind know it is occupied. Foxes and deer will leave scent which other members of the species will smell. Deer will also fray the bushes (stripping off the bark) with their antlers to show others they have been there.

▲ **Raccoons** (80 cm) Originating in America, these have now been brought to Europe and can be seen wild in some parts. Feed on fish which they catch in their paws.

▶ **Pine marten** (70 cm)

▲ **Bat** (60-80 mm)

▶ **Roe deer** (1.2 m) Live in small groups. Like all deer, only the male has antlers. Unlike horns, these are shed every year and new ones grown. The growing antlers are inside special skin called 'velvet', later rubbed off.

▼ **Fox** (1.1 m)

▼ **Wood mouse** (14 cm)

Fields and Hedgerows

Only a few mammals live out in open fields where there is little *cover* to protect them from enemies. Moles live under the ground in fields and do not come up very often. They are seldom seen, but mole hills show when they are present. These hills are heaps of soil thrown out as the mole burrows. Hares rely on their long back legs to run away quickly from their enemies in the open. When they lie still in a ploughed field, the colour of their fur makes them difficult to see.

Other mammals live in hedgerows and along woodland edges, feeding in fields. Rabbits often hide in burrows during the day and feed at night. Hedgehogs curl up in nests in hedges, waiting to come out at dusk. Many smaller mammals, such as voles, shrews and mice, live in long grass and bushes at the edge of fields. Because they are small, they need to eat all the time to stay alive and so they can be seen any time during the day. They hide from their enemies by making tunnels through the grass, to get to their feeding places. Large numbers of these small *rodents* (gnawing animals) cause damage by eating crops and tree bark. Larger animals (foxes, stoats and weasels) feed on them.

▼ **Rabbit** (45 cm) Ears have no black tips, unlike hare's ears.

▲ **Mole** (17 cm) Broad spadelike feet used for digging. Velvety fur can be brushed to lie in any direction.

▲ **Field Vole** (14 cm) Head broad, tail shorter than mouse's tail.

▲ **Shrew** (12 cm) Has long snout.

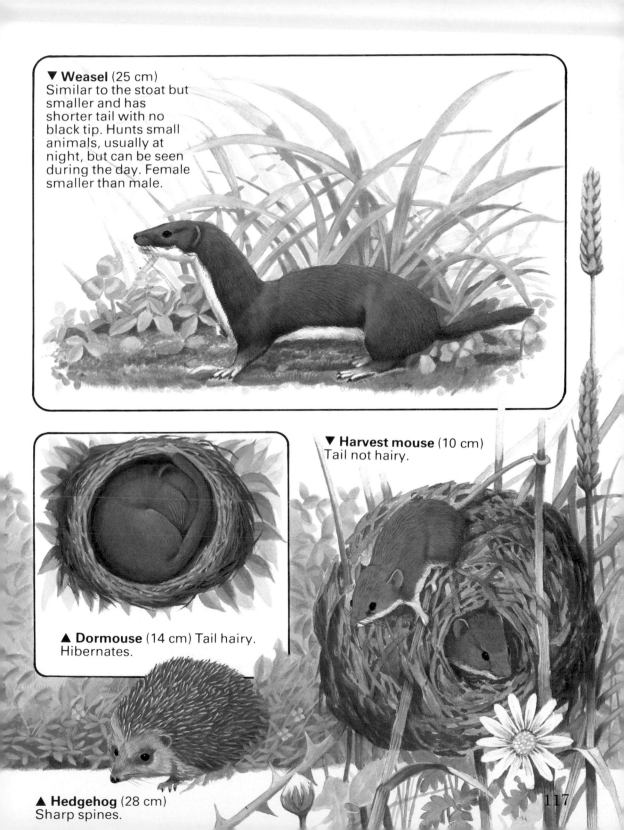

▼ **Weasel** (25 cm)
Similar to the stoat but
smaller and has
shorter tail with no
black tip. Hunts small
animals, usually at
night, but can be seen
during the day. Female
smaller than male.

▼ **Harvest mouse** (10 cm)
Tail not hairy.

▲ **Dormouse** (14 cm) Tail hairy.
Hibernates.

▲ **Hedgehog** (28 cm)
Sharp spines.

◄ Wild goats (1.5 m)
Many wild goats come from domestic goats that have bred in the wild. Animals that have escaped and live in the wild are called feral. Many so-called 'wild cats' are really feral

Goats live in herds led by an old male billy who has a beard. Both male and female have long curved horns. Colours vary between white, black and brown, or a mixture of these colours.

▼ Wild cat (90 cm)
The true wild cat has a bushy tail with broad black rings and a broad head. Lives in dens. Feeds on small creatures. Hunts at night.

► Mouflon (1.3 m)
Male: long curving horns; female: small ones. Both brown with a white back patch.

► Chamois (1.4 m) Both male and female have small horns turned back at tip. Brown with a black-and-white face.
Both these animals are found in Europe but not in Britain.

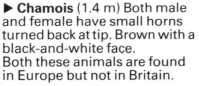

Hills and High Places

Few of the mammals that now live on hills and mountains really belong there, but the mountain hare is one that does. It turns white in winter, so that its enemies cannot see it easily. Its black ear tips are all that can be picked out against the white snow.

Many of the mammals living in the hills have been forced there by people who have hunted them and cut down the forests in which they lived before. In places where trees are being re-planted, mammals such as deer and wild cats are moving back to live.

Wild goats in the hills are descended from animals which were deliberately turned loose when sheep were farmed there. The goats ate the grass on dangerous ledges, so the less agile sheep were not tempted to try and reach it. Otherwise, these grazing sheep might have found themselves in a place from which they could not escape. They would have had either to starve or jump to their deaths.

◄ **Mountain hare** (67 cm) Ears shorter than brown hare. Digs small burrows.

▼ **Red deer** (2.65 m) Male has large spreading antlers. Lives in herds. Summer coat red-brown, winter coat grey.

▼ **Beaver** (1 m) A large animal with webbed feet and a broad, flat tail. Shy and difficult to see, usually coming out at night. Fells trees for food. Gnaws with sharp chisel-like teeth. Builds dams to keep water at a constant level. Builds 'lodges' above water, with entrance underwater. Found in Europe and North America, but extinct in Britain.

▲ **Otter** (1.12 m) Broad flat head and long tail. Sometimes lives near sea, especially in winter. Feeds on fish and small animals. The cubs are born in a burrow called a 'holt' and have to be taught to swim. The otter lies up by day, but at night keeps to a regular 'beat' up and down a river. Often also travels great distances overland.

▼ **Muskrat** (60 cm) Ponds, rivers.

European

American

Found in Europe.

▲ **Mink** (50 cm) Ponds, lakes.

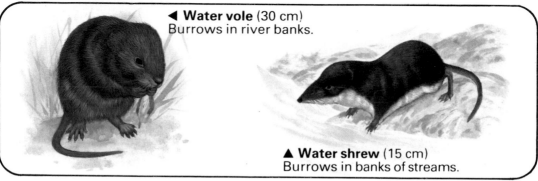

◀ **Water vole** (30 cm)
Burrows in river banks.

▲ **Water shrew** (15 cm)
Burrows in banks of streams.

Rivers and Lakes

Some mammals have made their homes in fresh water. They have *evolved* so that they can swim and find their food where there is not so much competition from other animals. Many water mammals have webs on their feet and use them as paddles. Their tails have become flattened so that the animals can use them for swimming. The beaver's tail is flattened from top to bottom, whilst the musk rat's is flattened sideways. Their body hair sheds the water easily, but they groom it to keep it waterproof.

Although they can swim under water, these mammals have to come to the surface to breathe, and most of their life is actually spent on land. Many of them live in burrows on the banks of rivers and ponds in which they feed. The young are born and looked after underground until they are old enough to learn to swim and look for food themselves. The burrow entrance is often under water but the actual home is not, so the helpless young will not be found by enemies. Sometimes burrows, like the musk rat's, cause such damage to river banks that they collapse.

Salt Water Mammals

Animals that live in sea water have become streamlined so that they can swim easily. Seals have smooth coats. Their front legs have become broad flippers and their hind legs form a 'tail' which sweeps from side to side to push them along. Seals have a layer of fat (*blubber*) under the skin to keep them warm. They hunt for fish under water, but have to come to the surface to breathe.

Seals come ashore to breed – the grey seal in autumn, the common seal in spring. Grey seal pups have white coats and stay on land for three weeks. Common seal pups can swim straight away.

Whales, too, have become streamlined. They have lost virtually all their hair except for a few bristles and so can move easily through the water. Their front legs have become flippers, but they have no hind legs. Instead, they have a large tail which pushes them along. The tail moves up and down, not from side to side like a fish's tail. Whales also have blubber under the skin to keep them warm. They breathe through *blow holes* on their heads and can store enough air to stay under water for some time.

There are two main kinds of whales, the whalebone (baleen) whale which feeds by sieving small animals through a fringe of bristles in its mouth, and the toothed whale which has teeth and feeds on fish. Baby whales are born, fed and looked after in the sea.

▼ **Grey seal** (3 m) Lives on rocky coasts. Has a broad flat head with no forehead. Feeds on fish.

▶ **Common seal** (1.5-2 m) Also called harbour seal. Lives near river mouths where there are sand-banks. Head narrow with a distinct forehead. Feeds on fish.

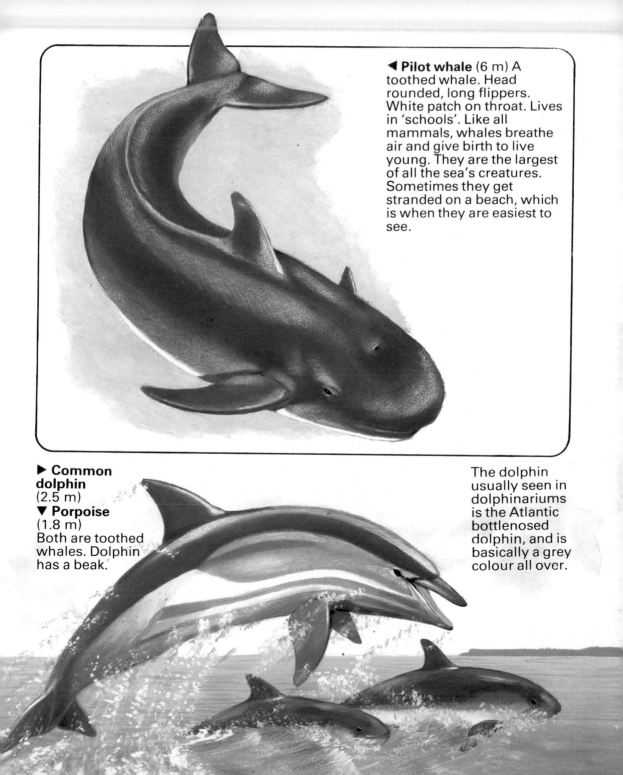

◄ Pilot whale (6 m) A toothed whale. Head rounded, long flippers. White patch on throat. Lives in 'schools'. Like all mammals, whales breathe air and give birth to live young. They are the largest of all the sea's creatures. Sometimes they get stranded on a beach, which is when they are easiest to see.

► Common dolphin (2.5 m)
▼ Porpoise (1.8 m)
Both are toothed whales. Dolphin has a beak.

The dolphin usually seen in dolphinariums is the Atlantic bottlenosed dolphin, and is basically a grey colour all over.

Index

Books to Read

Wild Flowers
The Nature Trail Book of Wild Flowers by Sue Tarsky (Usborne)
The Concise British Flora in Colour by W. Keble Martin (Michael Joseph)
Towns and Gardens by Denis Owen (Hodder & Stoughton)
The Pocket Encyclopedia of Wild Flowers by M. Christianson (Blandford)
The Wild Flowers of Britain and Northern Europe by R. Fitter, A. Fitter and M. Blamey (Collins)
Grasses by C. E. Hubbard (Penguin)
The Concise Flowers of Europe by Oleg Polunin (Oxford University Press)

Trees
Trees by Elizabeth Martin (Ward Lock)
A Field Guide to the Trees of Britain and Northern Europe by Alan Mitchell (Collins)
Trees and Bushes of Europe by Oleg Polunin and Barbara Everard (Oxford University Press)
The Illustrated Encyclopedia of Trees by Herbert Edlin and Maurice Nimmo (Salamander)
Spotter's Guide to Trees by Esmond Harris (Usborne)

Shells
Shells of the World by A. P. H. Oliver (Hamlyn)
Seashells by S. Peter Dance (Hamlyn)
Seashells of the World by Gert Linder (Blandford)
The Life of Animals with Shells by Solene Whybrow (Macdonald Educational)
The Observer's Book of Sea and Seashore Edited by I. O. Evans (Warne)
Collins Pocket Guide to the Seashore by John Barrett and C. M. Yonge (Collins)

Birds
Let's Look at Birds by Neil Ardley (Ward Lock)
The Nature Trail Book of Birdwatching by Malcolm Hart (Usborne)
The New Birdtable Book by Tony Soper (Pan)
The Oxford Book of Birds by Bruce Campbell (Oxford University Press)
The Observer's Book of Birds by S. Vere Benson (Warne)
A Field Guide to the Birds of Britain and Europe by R. Peterson, G. Mountfort and P. A. D. Hollom (Collins)

Insects
The Oxford Book of Insects by John Burton (Oxford University Press)
A Field Guide to the Insects of Britain and Northern Europe by Michael Chinery (Collins)
The Freshwater Life of the British Isles by John Clegg (Warne)
A Field Guide to the Butterflies of Britain and Europe by L. G. Higgins and N. D. Riley (Collins)
Towns and Gardens by Denis Owen (Rainbird)
The Nature Trail Book of Insect Watching by Ruth Thomson (Usborne)

Mammals
Collins Handguide to Wild Animals of Britain and Europe by D. Ovenden, G. Corbet and N. Arnold
The Observer's Book of Wild Animals by M. Burton (Warne)
A Field Guide to the Mammals of Britain and Europe by F. H. van den Brink (Collins)
British Mammals by L. Harrison Matthews (Collins)
The Handbook of British Mammals by Corbet and Southern (Blackwell)